POETRY

FOR BEGINNERS ®

POETRY
FOR BEGINNERS®

Margaret Chapman
Kathleen Welton

illustrations by *Reuben Negrón*

FOR BEGINNERS®

an imprint of Steerforth Press
Hanover, New Hampshire

For Beginners LLC
62 East Starrs Plain Road
Danbury, CT 06810 USA
www.forbeginnersbooks.com

A For Beginners® Documentary Comic Book
Copyright © 2010

Cataloging-in-Publication information is available from the Library of Congress.

ISBN # 978-1-934389-46-1 Trade

Manufactured in the United States of America

For Beginners® and Beginners Documentary Comic Books® are published by For Beginners LLC.

First Edition

10 9 8 7 6 5 4 3 2 1

If I read a book and it makes my whole body so cold no fire can ever warm me, I know that is poetry. If I feel physically as if the top of my head were taken off, I know that is poetry. These are the only ways I know it. Is there any other way?

Emily Dickinson, *Letters of Emily Dickinson*

Contents:

Chapter 1: I, Too, Dislike It

Poetry
Marianne Moore

I, too, dislike it: there are things that are important
beyond all this fiddle.
Reading it, however, with a perfect contempt for it,
one discovers that there is in
it after all, a place for the genuine.
(lines 1-5)

What Is Poetry?

Poetry is the journal of the sea animal living on land, wanting to fly in the air. Poetry is a search for syllables to shoot at the barriers of the unknown and the unknowable. Poetry is a phantom script telling how rainbows are made and why they go away.
—Carl Sandburg, from *Poetry Considered*

Poetry is life distilled.
—Gwendolyn Brooks

Poetry is not an expression of the party line. It's that time of night, lying in bed, thinking what you really think, making the private world public, that's what the poet does.
—Allen Ginsberg, from
Ginsberg: A Biography by Gary Miles

Poetry is whatever poetry can be.

Poetry can be what a young woman says when she steps up to a microphone and spills her guts, and moves the room.

Poetry can be the world, observed from a window, written down in secret.

Poetry can be whispered limericks in the back of the playground.

Or the verse a young playwright writes to immortalize his mistress, behind the back of his wife.

Or kids making up rhymes, trying to outdo each other.

Or it can be the secret language of revolutionaries and spies.

Or it can be truth spoken to power.

Or it can be, simply, a place for the genuine.

It is one of those things that can be a lot of things.

What poetry has always been is a way for millions of people across time to use language to try to better understand love, hate, war, religion, oppression, joy, sorrow, sex and death—the whole human condition.

So poetry is huge. Really, really enormous.

And it is all over the place. It is on birth announcements and on tombstones; at presidential inaugurations and high school graduations; on the radio and on the Internet. It is in textbooks and prayer books; in the Bible and the Torah and the Koran and the Tao Te Ching. Poetry is written in notebooks and journals. It is carved into the blocks of ancient tombs and written on bathroom walls.

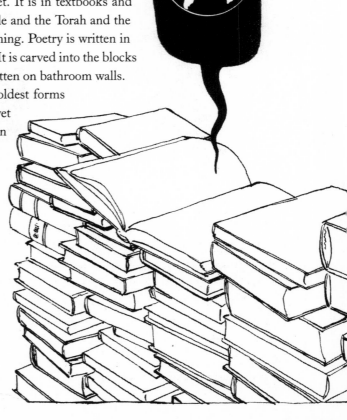

Poetry is one of the oldest forms of writing in the world, yet it is also fiercely modern and constantly evolving.

Poetry can be incredibly dense and complex, yet you probably learned to read by reading poetry.

Like many art forms, poetry is difficult to define. But let's try:

Poetry is writing that communicates intensely and intimately through and beyond language, using rhythm, sound, style and meaning.

Got it?

Poetry is intense, it is intimate, it uses language but it is more than just the words. It uses the rhythms, sounds, styles and meanings of the words to communicate.

We'll spend the rest of this book explaining exactly what that definition means.

That poetry is hard to define might be why some people find poetry intimidating. Many things we think of as part of "poetry"—emotion, love, rhyme, rhythm, line breaks, imagery—exist in lots of poetry, but certainly not all.

Which means that we can't tell you what poetry is by listing a set of component parts.

So let's look at what poetry does.

"A poet's work is to name the un-nameable, to point at frauds, to take sides, start arguments, shape the world, and stop it going to sleep."

—Salman Rushdie, novelist, *Independent* (London)

At its most basic level, poetry is a form of literature that focuses language's ability to **evoke** feelings, ideas, experiences, not just to transmit meaning. Poetry is writing that does more than just mean what the words themselves mean.

Because poetry can mean more than just the words as written, poets have often been on the forefront of political, cultural and intellectual change.

When you read a set of instructions, or an encyclopedia, the language you read was chosen by the author to convey a pretty precise meaning. We chose the words in the text of this book first and foremost to give you information.

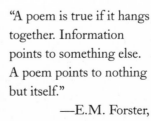

"A poem is true if it hangs together. Information points to something else. A poem points to nothing but itself."

—E.M. Forster, novelist, from *Two Cheers for Democracy* (1951)

While poets also want to engage and inform, poets look at language differently. Poets consider the sounds of words, the rhythms, the way words look on a page. They consider the symbolism of language, and the multiple meanings of words. They think about how the sounds and appearance of the words may affect you (the reader), how these things may trigger memories, or emotions, or images.

This means that not only does poetry contain the actual meaning of the words, but it contains a second meaning—it contains the meaning a reader gets from the poem.

So when you read a poem, you create the meaning of the poem. You are the one who makes the poem mean something. So for poetry to mean anything, you need to start reading it.

How Do You Read Poetry?

Try to love the questions themselves as if they were locked rooms or books written in a very foreign language.
—Rainer Maria Rilke, from *Letters to a Young Poet*, trans. Stephen Mitchell

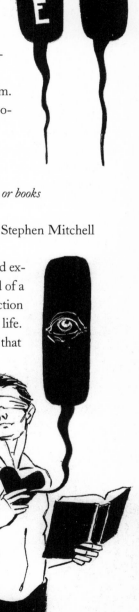

Like any sort of reading, poetry gives you access to ideas and experiences. When you read poetry, you get to peek into the mind of a poet, and see whether that person's experiences have any connection with your own, whether that person's ideas have a place in your life.

At some point in time, someone started spreading the rumor that to understand poetry, to know how to read poetry the "right way" you had to have all of this super-secret special insider knowledge about both poems and poets.

But that is just a rumor. Anyone can read any poem, anytime, anywhere. There is no super-secret insider knowledge. As long as you are fluent in the language the poem is written in, you can read it. And if you aren't fluent, you can probably find the poem in translation.

As you study poetry, you might gain information that changes the meaning you get from a poem, like what certain symbols might stand for, or which personal experiences a poet might be bringing into his or her work.

And while learning more about how a poem is created, and to what poets might be referring in their poems might make reading poetry more exciting, and give you new things to consider while reading, it doesn't make any meaning you get from a poem any more correct.

It might make it more fun.

Let's start reading.

Here's one of the most famous poems in the English language, Emily Dickinson's "Because I could not stop for Death—":

Because I could not stop for Death—(479)

Because I could not stop for Death—
He kindly stopped for me—
The Carriage held but just Ourselves—
And Immortality.

We slowly drove— He knew no haste
And I had put away
My labor and my leisure too,
For His Civility—

We passed the School, where Children strove
At Recess—in the Ring—
We passed the Fields of Gazing Grain—
We passed the Setting Sun—

Or rather—He passed Us—
The Dews drew quivering and Chill—
For only Gossamer, my Gown—
My Tippet— only Tulle—

We paused before a House that seemed
A Swelling of the Ground—
The Roof was scarcely visible—
The Cornice— in the Ground—

Shorter then—'tis Centuries—and yet
Feels shorter than the Day
I first surmised the Horses' Heads
Were toward Eternity—

Read it? Read it again. Out loud. We won't listen.

How did the poem sound? On its surface, this poem is deceptively straight-forward. Though it sounds simple, even childlike, it is complex and highly crafted. The words produce a rhythm that guides you as you read. Dickinson repeats vowel and consonant sounds, and even little phrases at the beginning of lines. Some-times she uses rhyme in expected places, sometimes she doesn't. But the rhythm is constant throughout.

Now say "Tippet only tulle" five times fast. A tippet is a shawl, and tulle is net-ting. Think about how "a shawl made of netting" is not nearly as fun to say as "Tippet only tulle."

She starts the poem with a little joke. Seems like she was going to miss her date with Death, but death went out of his way to meet up with her. How kind.

Emily Dickinson lived a solitary life, was never married and had no children. This poem seems to be her own reckoning with mortality; she imagines death as a journey to eternity. And it is hard not to think, with the poet in her gown and tulle, of a nineteenth century bride on her wedding day, being taken to her new house. Only this house is just "A Swelling of the Ground."

Notice how she uses dashes. That was Dickinson's trademark punctuation. Those dashes feel like they mean connection, not ending. So why does she end her poem with a dash? What comes after eternity?

Modern-day poet Billy Collins couldn't resist putting himself in the poem as Emily's groom. In "Taking Off Emily Dickinson's Clothes," he helps her with that tippet.

> First, her tippet made of tulle,
> easily lifted off her shoulders and laid
> on the back of a wooden chair.
> (lines 1-3)

Mortality is a common subject in poetry; Dickinson's poem is particularly effective because it combines humor with a kind fatalism or acceptance of death, and because these ideas play out in easy rhythm and simple images.

You should read the poem out loud one more time, after we picked it apart.

This is the unique capability of poetry—to combine the ideas, sounds, and the look of language in affecting and enticing ways, so that as we read poetry, the poem becomes not just the sum of its parts but an experience.

But over the course of history, poets have written in almost every possible way about almost every aspect of the human condition.

Which leads us to ask...

Where Did It Come From?

Poetry is one of the oldest forms of writing in the world. In fact, poetry is probably even older than writing itself.

The oldest known poetry was most likely sung, or chanted. Ancient poets used poetic techniques like rhyme and rhythm to make their poems easy to memorize.

The oldest known writings in the world are accounting and law codes—records of what people owned, and what they could and could not do. After people figured out the basic business of keeping track of things, they started using writing to record those poems they had been just memorizing and repeating for so long.

Example of poems that were probably written down long after they were first repeated:

The Epic of Gilgamesh, an ancient Mesopotamian poem about King Gilgamesh and his friend Enkido, is the oldest known poem, from around 2000 B.C.E.

Tablet X, column V

How, O how could I stay silent, how, O how could I keep quiet?
My friend whom I love has turned to clay:
Enkidu my friend whom I love has turned to clay.
Am I not like him? Must I lie down too,
Never to rise, ever again?

trans. Stephanie Dalley

The Hebrew Tanakh, and the Old Testament from which it is derived, are written in poetic forms. "The Song of Solomon" is a highly symbolic (and some say erotic) love poem.

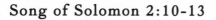

Song of Solomon 2:10-13

My beloved spoke, and said to me,
        "Rise up, my love, my beautiful one, and come away.
For, behold, the winter is past.
        The rain is over and gone.
The flowers appear on the earth.
        The time of the singing has come,
and the voice of the turtledove is heard in our land.
        The fig tree ripens her green figs.
The vines are in blossom.
        They give forth their fragrance.
Arise, my love, my beautiful one,
        and come away."

World English Bible

Homer's *Iliad* and *Odyssey* date from at least 900 B.C.E., and were recorded around 300 B.C.E. The *Iliad* focuses on Achilles and his struggle against Agamemnon during the attack on Troy. The *Odyssey* follows Odysseus (hence the name) and his ten year journey home from war to keep his wife Penelope from remarrying.

Book 5, 229-33

I long for home, long for the sight of home.
If any god has marked me out again
for shipwreck, my tough heart can undergo it.
What hardship have I not long since endured
at sea, in battle! Let the trial come.

trans. Robert Fitzgerald

Shi Jing (**Classic of Poetry or Book of Odes**), is a collection of poems said to have been edited by Confucius. The oldest surviving version is from around 200 BC, but some of the poems may be 1000 years older, like this one:

Chapter I, Section 9. Ode 7

Large rats, large rats, let us entreat
That you our millet will not eat.
But the large rats we mean are you,
With whom three years we've had to do,
And all that time have never known
One look of kindness on us thrown.
We take our leave of Wei and you;
That happier land we long to view.
O happy land! O happy land!
There in our proper place we'll stand.

trans. James Legge

Norse Poetic Eddas These poems about Norse gods and goddesses were probably sung all over Viking territory in the Dark Ages, before they were finally written down in Iceland in the thirteenth century.

In the poem "Hávamál," Odin explains the nature of love.

Poetic Edda, "Hávamál" 92-94

Soft words shall he speak | and wealth shall he offer
Who longs for a maiden's love,
And the beauty praise | of the maiden bright;
He wins whose wooing is best.

Fault for loving | let no man find
Ever with any other;
Oft the wise are fettered, | where fools go free,
By beauty that breeds desire.

Fault with another | let no man find
For what touches many a man;
Wise men oft | into witless fools
Are made by mighty love.

trans. Henry Adams Bellows

As poetry developed into a written form of literature, as opposed to a memorized form, people started reading it and then they started studying it, trying to figure out what was the best way to read it and what made a poem good or bad.

This sort of study is called **poetics**.

One of the first scholars of poetry, Aristotle (a Greek philosopher who had something to say about everything) wrote a sort of defense of poetry after his teacher, Plato, claimed that poetry was morally suspect.

In his book Poetics, Aristotle divided poetry into three categories: **Epic, Lyric** and **Dramatic**.

> **Epic** poetry told a long story, with an important hero.
> **Lyric** poetry was sung and accompanied by the lyre, hence the name.
> **Dramatic** poetry was performed as a play.

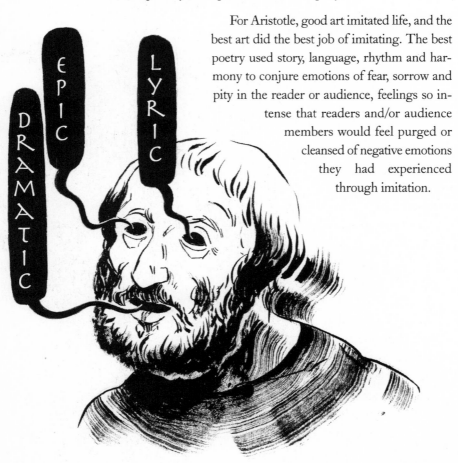

For Aristotle, good art imitated life, and the best art did the best job of imitating. The best poetry used story, language, rhythm and harmony to conjure emotions of fear, sorrow and pity in the reader or audience, feelings so intense that readers and/or audience members would feel purged or cleansed of negative emotions they had experienced through imitation.

Aristotle called this purge **catharsis**. This idea was the biggest in European and Middle Eastern poetics for more than 3000 years. Until John Keats.

(Between Aristotle and Keats were a number of very important poets and scholars with many ideas about poetry. We're skipping them for now.)

Right before Christmas, 1817, Keats wrote a letter to his brothers George and Thomas about how to read poetry. In the letter, Keats expressed his feeling that the best poetry is ambiguous and allows room for uncertainty.

Keats thought that poetry, more than any other art form, allowed space for the reader to feel unresolved, for meaning of the poems to remain somewhat mysterious, and that being okay with mysteries remaining mysteries was closer to the truth of life than Aristotle's all-wrapped-up big-finish explanations.

Keats called this sort of uncertainty **negative capability**.

Negative Capability, that is, when a man is capable of being in uncertainties, mysteries, doubts, without any irritable reaching after fact and reason.

—John Keats,
Selected Letters

You could think of the difference between catharsis and negative capability as the difference between watching an action blockbuster movie that leaves you exhilarated and watching an art house film that leaves you intrigued and uncertain.

For poems are not, as people think, simply emotions (one has emotions early enough)—they are experiences.
  —Rainer Maria Rilke, from *The Notebooks of Malte Laurids Brigge,* trans. Stephen Mitchell.

And poetry exists today that does both. Contemporary poetry runs the gamut from very traditional forms like odes and sonnets to young adult novels written entirely in free verse to found poetry to poetry that is so experimental it is impossible to be read aloud to spoken word and rap that can be improvised in the moment instead of written down at all.

And Who Is It for?

Because there are so
many types of poetry, trying to
do so many things, from expressing love to starting revolutions to dealing with
pain and sadness, there must be poems for everyone, in every circumstance. And
if there aren't, someone will write them.

Poets themselves can be anyone. Shakespeare was an actor. William Blake was
an engraver. Gabriela Mistral, Pablo Neruda and William Butler Yeats were politi-
cians. Poets Ted Kooser and Wallace Stevens were insurance agents, Walt Whit-
man was a government clerk, and William
Carlos Williams was a pediatrician. Queen
Elizabeth I wrote sonnets; so did soldier
and privateer Sir Walter Raleigh.

POETS CAN BE ANYONE.

Musicians Bob Dylan, Leonard Cohen
and Patti Smith have had their lyrics included
in poetry anthologies, as have rappers Public
Enemy, Wu Tang Clan, Tupac Shakur and Jay Z, among others.

But, really, any kid who has ever tried to rap has been composing poetry. Whether
you call it rap or poetry probably depends on who you are trying to impress.

In the Italian Renaissance, writing love sonnets was a great way to pick up girls. In nineteenth century England, writing poetry was a way for young aristocrats to rebel against stifling social expectations (and to pick up girls).

It has also been a way for people to express unpopular views, across history.

In fact, poets have often been on the forefront of social change. They have written about and supported issues such as equal rights for women, minorities and gays long before it was fashionable or even socially acceptable. They have invented new words when the words they wanted did not exist, and created new forms when existing forms were too constraining. They look to the past and across cultural boundaries for inspiration, making connections between people across time and space. Poets stretch the boundaries of language and help create new worlds.

How do they do all that? With poetry.
And how does poetry do all that?
Let's see.

Chapter 2: Getting at the Meaning of Poems

Song of Myself
Walt Whitman

Have you reckoned a thousand acres much? Have you reckoned the earth much?
Have you practiced so long to learn to read?
Have you felt so proud to get at the meaning of poems?

Stop this day and night with me and you shall possess the origin of all poems,
You shall possess the good of the earth and sun. . . . there are millions of suns left,
You shall no longer take things at second or third hand. . . . nor look through the eyes of the dead.
*   nor feed on the spectres in books,*
You shall not look through my eyes either, nor take things from me,
You shall listen to all sides and filter them from yourself.

(lines 30-37)

Poetry is one of the most intimate forms of communication between writer and reader.

It's like a message sealed in a bottle, or tied to a balloon, or tossed into a time machine, by a poet hopeful that somewhere, sometime, somehow, a stranger will read it and make a connection, find a meaning.

Sometimes this message is a whispered sweet nothing, sometimes it is a scream caught and pressed into paper, sometimes it is a sob or a sigh or a sinking feeling in the pit of your stomach. Always it is someone trying to make something new, to explore ideas and thoughts and feelings in the way only poetry and poets can.

And some poets are lucky. Their work is good enough and liked enough that it does get read by people they've never met, sometimes years or even centuries after they wrote it. People find their writing, their little messages, and they try to decode them.

Why is it hard to figure out what it means? Shouldn't they just say what they mean?

One thing about poetry – remember we said "you make the meaning in poetry?" This chapter will illustrate some common poetic techniques. Understanding and recognizing these techniques help you make that meaning.

Some poetry is very straight forward. But one of the most exiting aspects of poetry is that it is often trying to say something that is hard to say, to describe something that is almost indescribable. Poetry is trying to get at things—feelings, ideas, experiences—which are hard to be straightforward about.

The Meaning of a Poem

One of the things poetry often tries to deal with is **abstraction**. Abstractions are ideas, feelings, images, that are hard to pin down. One reason to use poetry to deal with abstraction is poetry has a special relationship to language that makes it possible to try to look at, to get at, things in new and exciting and sometimes difficult ways.

Poetry is a quite radical use of language, because it asks readers to look at words in a different way than when we are just reading for comprehension. Poetry makes readers do work, instead of just being spoon-fed things like "a point" or "an idea" - poetry gestures to many ideas, it combines meaning with ambiguity, allows space for readers to bring their own emotional, historical, political, mythological, spiritual, what-ever-else connections to language into the meaning of a poem.

Poetry is not willfully obtuse, or difficult, although it is occasionally difficult to make meaning from at first glance. Poetry, good poetry, teaches you how to read it as you read it. At first you may notice patterns of rhyme and rhythm, or line length. You may see that the poem has breaks in it. You may notice that the poet creates images, or references things outside of the poem, or tries to create an overall mood. Recognizing these things help you to go deeper into the poem.

Part of understanding poetry is being okay with not always finding a precise, or unlocked, meaning in a poem. Ambiguity in poetry is often "par for the course", and sometimes the meaning in poetry can't be parsed out, or explained in ways different from those that the poet explained it originally. If you could say, or write, the same thing a different way, and it would mean exactly the same thing, then it probably isn't a very good poem to begin with.

So if meaning in poetry isn't totally set, and how do you know if you have "gotten" a poem. Emily Dickinson said it was when she felt as if "the top of my head were taken off." If you are not as hard-core as Dickinson, there are a few other ways to know if you have gotten a poem:

- If you read a poem and you like it, you've probably "gotten it."

- If you read a poem and react physically—your heart tightens, or your eyes well up, or you realize that you had started holding your breath, or you feel as if the top of your head comes off.

- If you read a poem a few times, and eventually you start to think, "Okay, I see now, I think I know what the poet was going for here."

When starting to read poetry, you should look at three main aspects of a poem. Knowing a little bit about them will help you start attacking a poem and getting at its meaning:

The look of a poem
The sound of a poem
The sense of a poem

Some poems have a look and sound that rigidly conforms to a predetermined set of rules—these rules are called poetic **Forms**. The next chapter will cover a lot of these in depth.

The Look of a Poem

One of the quickest and easiest ways to tell a poem from another form of writing is simply to look at one on the page.

Forgetfulness
Hart Crane

Forgetfulness is like a song
That, freed from beat and measure, wanders.
Forgetfulness is like a bird whose wings are reconciled,
Outspread and motionless, —
A bird that coasts the wind unwearyingly.

Forgetfulness is rain at night,
Or an old house in a forest, — or a child.
Forgetfulness is white, — white as a blasted tree,
And it may stun the sybil into prophecy,
Or bury the Gods.

I can remember much forgetfulness.

Does it look like a poem? It probably is.

And how does it look like a poem? For the most part, and there certainly are exceptions, poetry is formatted differently than prose. Most simply put, poets do not write all the way to the edge of the page. They stop somewhere before the edge, and the words that are on the same line on the page are called, simply, **a line**.

Forgetfulness is like a song

And a group of lines together is called a **stanza**, which comes from Latin (to stand) and from Italian (a room). Like a room, a stanza can come in different shapes and sizes.

Forgetfulness is like a song
That, freed from beat and measure, wanders.
Forgetfulness is like a bird whose wings are reconciled,
Outspread and motionless, —
A bird that coasts the wind unwearyingly.

The line is the most important distinction between poetry and prose. If you take a paragraph of prose, and say, change the font size, or the width of the paper, so that you change the number of lines of text, you have not messed with the meaning of the paragraph. You've just changed the look. However, if you change which words fall on a line in poetry, you have changed the meaning of the poem. It isn't even the same poem any more.

Why? Why does the meaning change?

In regular prose writing, a writer has a set of punctuation to use to help the reader to understand when the writer is moving from one complete thought to another, or making a list, or trying to connect things. Poets not only have punctuation, and the rules that go a long with it, they also have the **line break**. The line break forces you to take a pause, and pausing in reading is a time to think about things. Poetry has the ability to make you stop and think about things in places you might otherwise not.

The places where the poet decides to stop writing on one line and move to the next are called **line breaks**.

One of the earliest reason for making poems with line breaks was to create lines with matching rhythm and rhyme, to indicate to the reader how the poem was to be read.

To My Dear and Loving Husband
Anne Bradstreet

If ever two were one, then surely we.
If ever man were loved by wife, then thee;
If ever wife was happy in a man,
Compare with me ye women if you can.
I prize thy love more than whole mines of gold,
Or all the riches that the East doth hold.
My love is such that rivers cannot quench,
Nor ought but love from thee give recompense.
Thy love is such I can no way repay;
The heavens reward thee manifold, I pray.
Then while we live, in love let's so persever,
That when we live no more we may live ever.

In Anne Bradstreet's poem, the rhyming words are at the end of the line, as are the majority of the punctuation marks. Bradstreet also keeps her line lengths about the same.

When you read the poem, you usually make a little pause at the end of each line. This means you have a little break before the first word of each line and after the last word—that gives the first and last words of the lines a little more importance than the words in the middle.

The lines in Langston Hughes's poem "Let America Be America Again" don't have an equal number of syllables, but they do have rhymes at the end of the lines.

Let America be America again.
Let it be the dream it used to be.
Let it be the pioneer on the plain
Seeking a home where he himself is free.

(lines 1-4)

In Christina Rossetti's poem "Who Has Seen the Wind?" she isn't as concerned with keeping the rhyme at the end of the line as Anne Bradstreet or Langston Hughes. She ends most of her lines on a punctuation mark, which are natural places for readers to make a pause.

Who has seen the wind?
Neither I nor you.
But when the leaves hang trembling,
The wind is passing through.
Who has seen the wind?
Neither you nor I.
But when the trees bow down their heads,
The wind is passing by.

What happens when you read each line in this stanza of Robert Creeley's "A Wicker Basket" on its own:

So that's you, man,
or me. I make it as I can,
I pick up, I go
faster than they know—

(lines 9-12)

Creeley changes direction after each line break. The first line is about "you, man." But taken with the second line, it is really about "us" (you or me.) The third line seems to be about leaving - picking up and going implies skipping town, maybe. But that "faster" in fourth line changes the meaning of both "picking up" and "going:" this poem is about speed now, and about under-estimation. The last thought in this stanza is "I go faster than they know—." By the end it seems like he is getting away with something.

If you notice in the Bradstreet and Hughes poems, not only did they rhyme at the end of the line, they also repeated the first word of the line. Using line breaks to create repetition at the beginning of the line is called **anaphora**, from the Greek word for repeat.

Here are the first few lines of N. Scott Momaday's "The Delight Song of Tsoai-Talee":

I am a feather on the bright sky
I am the blue horse that runs in the plain
I am the fish that rolls, shining, in the water
I am the shadow that follows a child

(lines 1-4)

Reading the same line or word or sound more than once, whether in a refrain or a rhyme, takes the poem and the reader outside of the realm of everyday written language. The repetition in these lines anchors each line and at the same time sets off the images – we begin to read over the meaning of the words "I am," but we hear it in our heads like a drum.

The Sound of a Poem

Earlier we said a poem looks like a poem. Often, a poem sounds like a poem too. In fact, there have been many people throughout history who believed that "sounding good" was the most important aspect of a poem.

There are lots of techniques poets use to make a poem sound good. The two most common are probably rhythm and rhyme, but others often used are alliteration, consonance and assonance.

Every poem basically exists two ways—it exists on the page, and it exists read out loud. Some poems do better one way or another—concrete poetry and experimental poetry sometimes can't be read out loud. Other types of poems, especially poems that use rhyme and rhythm, or play with the sound of language, might seem better when they are heard than when they are read.

Many people think of **rhyme** when they first think of poetry.

The simple definition of **rhyme** is when two or more words have the same ending sound. Rhymes sometimes have the same written ending, but because English spelling is all over the place, often words rhyme even if they look completely different.

For example:

Ease
Breeze

Orange
Blorenge (a place in Wales)

Rhyme is a little more complicated than just the same ending sound - there are two sorts of rhyme. Perfect rhymes also have to have the same pattern of stress on the syllables.

For example:

Beautiful
Dutiful

Another common type of rhyme in poetry is **slant rhyme**. Slant rhyme is when words sound similar, but don't actually rhyme. Slant rhyme actually encompasses a few different literary techniques, including **half rhyme**, when the final consonant sounds match, **consonance**, when most of the consonant sounds match, **assonance**, when just the vowel sounds match, and sometimes even **alliteration**, when the first sounds of the word match. Alliteration and assonance are often used in poems that don't rhyme, as well.

Although sometimes poets use slant rhyme when they can't find a perfect rhyme for a word, slant rhyme is also often used just to play with the sound of the poem.

Lines Written in Dejection
William Butler Yeats

When have I last looked on
The round green eyes and the long wavering bodies·
Of the dark leopards of the moon?
All the wild witches, those most noble ladies,
For all their broom-sticks and their tears,
Their angry tears, are gone.

The holy centaurs of the hills are vanished;
I have nothing but the embittered sun;
Banished heroic mother moon and vanished,
And now that I have come to fifty years
I must endure the timid sun.

Here, Yeats, uses **half rhyme**: **bodies** and **ladies** both end with the "-dies" sound.

Yeats also uses alliteration—notice all the "l" and "w" sounds in this poem.

In contemporary poetry, slant rhyme is very important in spoken word, slam poetry and hip hop. Slant rhyme is probably the most important kind of rhyme in rap. Read these lyrics from Wu-Tang Clan's "Triumph" out loud:

> I bomb atomically, Socrates' philosophies
> and hypothesis can't define how I be droppin these
> mockeries.

There is a very impressive string of slant rhymes: atomically, philosophies, hypothesis, droppin these, and mockeries.

There is another, more radical form of rhyme, called visual rhyme, or sometimes eye rhyme. This in when two words that sound nothing alike look like they should rhyme on the page:

For example, slaughter and laughter.

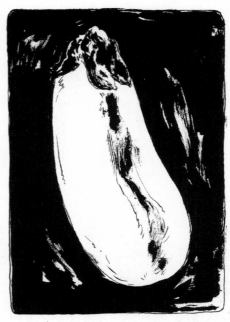

EGGPLANT   YELLOW SQUASH

When you read rhyming poetry you probably notice that the rhyme often follows a pattern. This pattern is called a rhyme scheme, and it has to do with which lines in the poem rhyme with each other.

When studying poetry, people like to notate the rhyme scheme. You do this by assigning a letter to each rhyme sound, and then you list the letters in order of the rhyme. Let's try with the first stanza of William Wordsworth's "I Wandered Lonely as a Cloud":

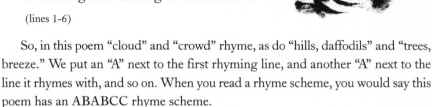

> I wandered lonely as a cloud A
> That floats on high o'er vales and hills, B
> When all at once I saw a crowd, A
> A host, of golden daffodils; B
> Beside the lake, beneath the trees, C
> Fluttering and dancing in the breeze. C

(lines 1-6)

So, in this poem "cloud" and "crowd" rhyme, as do "hills, daffodils" and "trees, breeze." We put an "A" next to the first rhyming line, and another "A" next to the line it rhymes with, and so on. When you read a rhyme scheme, you would say this poem has an ABABCC rhyme scheme.

By the way, have you noticed that in most rhyming poems, the rhyming words are at the end of the line? This is called **end rhyme**. Rhyme schemes really only refer to where the end rhyme is in a poem. Rhymes that don't occur at the end of the line are called **internal rhyme**.

Probably the most common sort of rhyme scheme is when two rhyming lines are right next to each other. These are called **rhyming couplets**.

Here's an example, "Song of the Witches," from Shakespeare's *Macbeth*, (which is a play full of poetry):

> Double, double toil and trouble; A
> Fire burn and caldron bubble. A
> Fillet of a fenny snake, B
> In the caldron boil and bake; B
> Eye of newt and toe of frog, C
> Wool of bat and tongue of dog, C
> Adder's fork and blind-worm's sting, D
> Lizard's leg and howlet's wing, D
> For a charm of powerful trouble, E
> Like a hell-broth boil and bubble. E

So every two lines rhyme together in pairs.If you were discussing this rhyme scheme, you would probably just call it an AABB scheme—you sort of get the point after the first few couplets. In this section there is a ton of end rhyme, but also some internal rhyme, especially in that first line.

If you haven't already, try reading this section from *Macbeth* out loud. Notice anything? You might notice the repetition—there is a load of alliteration in these few lines. You may also notice that the words seem a little sing-songy? Maybe you find yourself reading to a certain beat?

Can you hear the rhythm in the poem?

Let's talk about that. Rhythm in poetry can come from repetition, like anaphora or alliteration, or from something called meter. Meter is a pattern of stressed and unstressed syllables in poetry which is constant throughout a number of lines, or an entire poem.

All words have syllables that are either stressed or unstressed. Think of the word "syllables." We pronounce it SYLL-a-bles. It would sound weird if we pronounced it syll-A-bles.

When we are looking at meter in poems, we look for two or three syllable patterns which are repeated. These are called feet.

When we have a consistent pattern of stressed and unstressed syllables, we get a rhythm in the language.

Let's go back to Shakespeare again. Let's look at the first line of one of his most famous sonnets, Sonnet 18, and write out the pattern of stressed syllables as a series of "da"—unstressed, and "DUM"—stressed.

Shall	I	com-	pare	thee	to	a	sum-	mer's	day?
Da	DUM	da	DUM	da	DUM	da	DUM	da	DUM

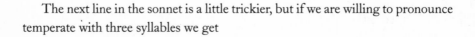

The next line in the sonnet is a little trickier, but if we are willing to pronounce temperate with three syllables we get

Thou	art	more	love-	ly	and	more	tem-	pe-	rate.
Da	DUM	da	DUM	da	DUM	da	DUM	da	DUM

This **pattern** here—the "Da DUM da DUM da DUM da DUM da DUM"
—is the most famous meter in English poetry. It's called `iambic pentameter`.
An iamb is a two-syllable **foot** where the second syllable is stressed, and pen-
tameter means it is repeated five times.

Types of feet

Two Syllable Feet
Iamb (Iambic) da DUM
Trochee (Trochaic) DUM da
Spondee (Spondaic) DUM DUM

Three Syllable Feet
Anapest (Anapestic) da da DUM
Dactyl (Dactylic) DUM da da

Meter Lengths

Monometer: One foot
Dimeter: Two feet
Trimeter: Three feet
Tetrameter: Four feet
Pentameter: Five feet
Hexameter: Six feet
Heptameter: Seven feet
Octameter: Eight feet

Figuring out the exact name for the meter in a poem isn't really that important, except to know that some poetic forms always use a specific meter.

But just for fun, can you figure out the meter of the first two lines of the "Song of The Witches?"

Trochaic Tetrameter! You were right!

Moving on.

Contemporary poetry sometimes has a standard meter, and at other times doesn't have a set meter but still has a rhythm to it.

Much like the syncopated rhythms of jazz drummers, contemporary poets use the stresses in language to make complicated rhythms, which in turn, change how you read the poem.

Thirteen Ways of Looking at a Blackbird
Wallace Stevens

VIII

I know noble accents
And lucid, inescapable rhythms;
But I know, too,
That the blackbird is involved
In what I know.

Try reading this out loud a few times. Think about what words you stress when you read it. Look for repetition in the lines and in the stanza.

The first, third and fifth line all have the words "I know" in them. But he doesn't put them on the beginning of every line - in fact these "I knows" seem to be drifting across the page - first at the beginning, then the middle, then the end. He is creating rhythm here, but it isn't as straightforward as iambic pentameter. Neither is the rythm in Nikki Giovanni's "Quilts":

No longer do I cover tables filled with food and laughter
My seams are frayed my hems falling my strength no longer able
To hold the hot and cold

(lines 3-5)

These lines have a very strong rhythm, although it changes from line to line. Giovanni uses syllable patterns, internal rhyme, slant rhyme, repetition and alliteration in order to make a compelling rhythm that makes you want to read these lines out loud.

The Sense of a Poem

The look and sound of a poem together contribute to the meaning of the poem. But not only do poets have the look of the poem and the sound of the poem, they have the meanings and ideas behind the words. Sometimes poets use words in a very straightforward way, but most often in poetry, language is doing more work that just describing one thing, or telling one story.

Take the first three lines of Lucille Clifton's poem "at last we killed the roaches":

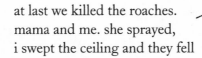

at last we killed the roaches.
mama and me. she sprayed,
i swept the ceiling and they fell

These lines present a pretty straightforward, if sort of horrifying for the roach-phobic, scene of killing roaches. Notice the alliteration of *sprayed, swept* and *ceiling*, and of *mama* and *me*. Notice the first and last words on each line, the quick succession of *roaches, sprayed* and *fell*.

In these first few lines, Clifton is using **imagery**, the technique of describing an image (or even a sound, a smell, or a feeling) so that the reader can visualize (or hear, or smell, or feel) what the poet is talking about. In this poem she uses **concrete imagery**—describing a very specific thing that happened. Poets also use **abstract imagery**—which describes more things in a less specific way. For example the specific sense of "a time of war," or "it was a beautiful night," would depend on what a reader thought about of war or beauty.

Now read those lines in the context of the rest of the poem.

at last we killed the roaches
Lucille Clifton

at last we killed the roaches.
mama and me. she sprayed,
i swept the ceiling and they fell
dying onto our shoulders, in our hair
covering us with red. the tribe was broken,
the cooking pots were ours again
and we were glad, such cleanliness was grace
when i was twelve. only for a few nights,
and then not much, my dreams were blood
my hands were blades and it was murder murder
all over the place.

In the context of the whole poem, the meaning of that initial event changes. The twelve-year-old is conflicted—she wants the cleanliness, but she is also haunted by destroying this "tribe." The roaches stop being horrible pests, the act of killing them, because she calls it murder, is compared to the act of killing people. The words she has chosen, like "cleanliness" might remind us of the idea of "ethnic cleansing." And though she is haunted, she is only haunted "for a few nights." Clifton is writing about our ability to feel deeply but still to forget.

So that initial description went on to be much more than it is. Poets have a number of tools for making more meaning from language.

The first and most important tool poets have is **word choice**— picking words that fit the poem. If Lucille Clifton had chosen the word "killing," instead of "murder" her poem would not have been comparing the roaches to people. This is because, although the words have similar meaning, they have different **connotation**.

The connotation of a word is the subtler meanings of a word, the emotional or cultural meanings. "Killing" and "murder" can mean the same thing, but usually we only talk about murdering a person, not an animal. Another example is the difference between the words "house" and "home." A home connotes a certain coziness, a sense of family and history. A house might be just a dwelling.

So when you are talking about words having shades of meaning, connotation is a pretty mild example. The more extreme kind is called figurative language.

Figurative language means something different from what is literally said. While we use figurative language in ordinary speech, figurative language is the poet's most powerful tool. Although there are plenty of poems that do not use figurative language, most poets find that figurative language opens up more possibilities in the poems.

The most common sort of figurative language is **metaphor.** Metaphor is a comparison of two unlike things that have a common aspect, for example:

He is a pig.

That car is a lemon.

fig. A: Pig.   fig B: Lemon.

The first example probably makes you think of a person who eats a lot. That's what "he" has in common with a pig—they both have big appetites, and are messy. We are probably not at a farm, pointing at a barn-yard animal and explaining what kind of animal it is.

So "he" isn't literally a pig.

Also the car isn't actually a lemon. That would be weird.

A lemon is a bitter fruit that looks tastier than it is. The car looks good but it doesn't work right.

These two metaphors are so common that the metaphoric meaning is now one of the definitions of the word.

Metaphors don't have to be "a _____ is a _____." They can also occur when you put an action with an object in a sort of impossible way.

Throw some light on the problem.

First, you can't throw light. Second, there is probably no actual light involved. Throwing light is a visual metaphor meaning to show, in detail, what is going on, like turning on a light in a room.

What about **similes**?

Right. A simile is a basically metaphor that uses the words "like," or "as." The main difference between metaphor and simile is that a simile usually tells exactly what kind of comparison is being made, where as metaphors may have many points of comparison.

I'm as corny as Kansas in August

Like a rolling stone

However, not every phrase with like or as is a simile:

As I was saying, I like Kansas in August.

Sly like a fox.

Another type of comparison related to metaphor is **metonym**— when refering to something using a different word that what you actually mean.

A head-count

The White House denied reports that aliens had taken over the country.

A head count means a whole person count. The White House actually means someone from the President's staff.

In the first lines of her poem "Morning Song," Sylvia Plath uses metonym and simile to compress the timeframe of conception and birth:

> Love set you going like a fat gold watch.
> The midwife slapped your footsoles, and your bald cry
> Took its place among the elements.

(lines 1-3)

Love stands in for conception, and the watch is a simile for pregnancy. The slap and the cry are metonym for birth. Quick and easy.

Poets also use metaphors that built off each other, called **extended metaphors**. In Pablo Neruda's "Ode to the Watermelon," he describes what happens when you cut into the fruit:

> its hemispheres open
> showing a flag
> green, white, red,
> that dissolves into
> wild rivers, sugar,
> delight!

(lines 36-41)
trans. Robert Bly

Neruda is making lots of comparisons in this short stanza. He compares the whole watermelon to the globe, by calling its halves hemispheres. He compares the green, white and red interior of the watermelon to a flag, and the juice running out of the melon to a "wild river." And though these are three distinct metaphors, they are thematically similar—globe, flag, river. He is talking about geography.

Related to metaphor are the poetic tools **symbol** and **allusion**. A **symbol** is an object or image that represents, or stands for, something else. We use symbols all the time in everyday life. Think of an octagon. An octagon does necessarily mean anything other than an eight sided shape; however when you see an octagon—especially a red octagon— you know it means STOP. Sometimes symbols are so common we almost forget they are symbols.

One important thing about a symbol is that a symbol's meaning is not always constant. A skull and crossbones on a sign, or on a bottle, means poison or danger, but when it is white on a black flag it repre- sents pirates, especially playful, movie-like pirates.

A second important aspect of symbols is that they are often arbitrary. There is nothing inherent in an octagon that makes it a stop-worthy shape. Stop signs could have been hexagons, or trapezoids. The symbol gets it's meaning because people agree it means something.

A symbol and a metaphor can be very simi- lar. Edna St. Vincent Millay uses the symbol of a candle, and creates a metaphor with it, in her poem "First Fig":

First Fig

My candle burns at both ends;
    It will not last the night;
But ah, my foes, and oh, my friends—
    It gives a lovely light!

A candle is a common symbol for a person's life. She extends the symbol by imagining burning both ends at once – a concrete image and a visual metaphor for how tricky it is to do too much and live too fast.

Similar to symbol, an **allusion** refers to something other than itself, such as a well-known event, story or myth. When a poet uses an allusion, or alludes to a well-known story, the poet wants you to bring your knowledge of that story into the poem.

Let's look in-depth at the first stanza of John Keats's "Ode on Melancholy":

No, no, go not to Lethe, neither twist
  Wolf's-bane, tight-rooted, for its poisonous wine;
Nor suffer thy pale forehead to be kiss'd
  By nightshade, ruby grape of Proserpine;
    Make not your rosary of yew-berries,
  Nor let the beetle, nor the death-moth be
    Your mournful Psyche, nor the downy owl
A partner in your sorrow's mysteries;
  For shade to shade will come too drowsily,
    And drown the wakeful anguish of the soul.

(lines 1-10)

This stanza is packed with symbol and allusion, and the poem would be hard, if not impossible, to understand without knowing what Keats is referring to here. Here's a quick glossary:

Symbols:

Melancholy is sadness or depression. Keats is writing about melancholy, but he is writing to a person who is suffering from this disease.

Lethe is a river in the Greek underworld that one crosses after death; it causes the dead to forget their previous life, cares and attachments.

Wolf's bane is a poisonous root, which Keats asks us not to drink,

Nightshade, or Deadly Night-shade, has small, purple poison-ous flowers that Keats calls "ruby grapes of Proserpine."

Yew is a shrub with poisonous leaves.

The **beetle**, or scarab, is Egyptian symbol of death.

The **death-moth**, or Death's-head Hawk moth, is a large European moth with a skull-like pattern on its back. It has been associated with death since the Middle Ages, and more recently was the moth in the film "Silence of the Lambs."

The **owl** is connect to funerals and death, as well as to the night, darkness, and ghosts because of its spooky call.

So far for symbols we have the river of death, deadly plants, creepy animals.

Allusions

Proserpine, more commonly called Persephone, was the daughter of the Greek earth goddess Demeter. She was kidnapped by Hades, king of the underworld, and made Queen and goddess. She rules the world of the dead.

Psyche was originally a mortal woman who was so beautiful that Eros (or Cupid) fell in love with her. Psyche was sent by Eros's mother, Aphrodite, into the underworld to steal some of Persephone's beauty and is one of the few mortals to enter the underworld and return alive. Although the word "psyche" now often refers to a person's personality, or even their soul, Psyche the goddess was an object of obsession for her husband Eros.

For allusions we have Proserpine, Queen of the Underworld, and Psyche, the victim of obsessive love.

After figuring out what the specific symbols and allusions mean—they all have something to do with poison, the underworld, death or obsession—can you start to get some sort of meaning out of the poem?

Keats asks the reader not to go to the river of death, not to drink poison, which is Proserpine's drink. He asks us not to let "the death-moth be Your mournful Psyche": he's making an allusion Psyche's lonely journey to the underworld, her association with the soul, and her role as an object of obsession.

He is asking the reader not to be obsessed with death, not to drink poison.

He is saying don't commit suicide.

As he is talking about depression, he uses symbols from nature and allusions to Greek mythology. Why?

Partly because that was the style of poetry in the nineteenth century, and partly because using symbols and allusions connects poetry to something larger than itself. Keats is certainly not trying to be obscure. He most likely would have assumed that most of his readers would already know the meaning of the symbols he was using.

Contemporary poets may use contemporary symbols, like brands or place names, they may use allusions to film stars or TV shows or pop-songs, but they may also allude to well-known stories.

Finally, one of the things that poets and readers need to keep in mind is something that is a combination of the look, and the sound, and the meaning of the poem. It comes from word choice, from the form of the poem, from how line breaks and stanza breaks are used, from rhythm and rhyme, as well as from which kinds of images or descriptions are in the poem. It's called tone, and it is the overall feeling over everything in the poem together.

In the first section of T.S. Eliot's "Preludes" he sets the tone of the poem with his description of a lonely and neglected urban streetscape:

I
The winter's evening settles down
With smell of steaks in passageways.
Six o'clock.
The burnt-out ends of smoky days.
And now a gusty shower wraps
The grimy scraps
Of withered leaves across your feet
And newspapers from vacant lots;
The showers beat
On empty blinds and chimney-pots,
And at the corner of the street
A lonely cab-horse steams and stamps.
And then the lighting of the lamps.

(lines 1-13)

If the tone is the feeling of a poem, the **theme** is the overall idea of the poem, or what the poem is about. Like much about poetry, identifying themes isn't an exact science.

Poetry is written about all themes, and lots of poetry has more than one subject; in fact, much poetry has an upfront subject, or primary thing the poem is about, as well as a **subtext**, or secondary subject or idea. If you look back at Lucille Clifton's "at last we killed the roaches" the subject is killing roaches. But the "murder" of roaches brings up a subtext of mass killings of people.

While the subject of a poem is the topic the poem, the theme of a poem is the aspect of the subject that the poet is trying to explore. A love poem might be about the enduring nature of love, or about love that changes over time; it might be about be about love lost or love not yet attained. A poem on nature could explore the beauty of nature, or the destructive power of nature, or the battles between nature and industry.

Love and Marriage
"How Do I Love Thee? Let Me Count the Ways" by Elizabeth Barrett Browning
"She Walks in Beauty" by George Gordon, Lord Byron
"The Good-Morrow" by John Donne
"Having a Coke with You" by Frank O'Hara
"To Sylvia, To Wed" by Robert Herrick
"i carry your heart with me" by E.E. Cummings

Rejection and Breakups
"Love's Secret" by William Blake
"Why should a foolish marriage vow" by John Dryden
"For My Lover, Returning To His Wife" by Anne Sexton
"The Realization of Difference" by Diane Wakowski

Death and Loss
"A Valediction: Forbidding Mourning" by John Donne
"Out, Out" by Robert Frost
"Verses Upon the Burning of our House" by Anne Bradstreet
"One Art" by Elizabeth Bishop

Nature
"I Wandered Lonely as a Cloud (The Daffodils)" by William Wordsworth
"Nothing to Save" by D.H. Lawrence

"Arbolé, Arbolé" by Federico García Lorca
"13 Ways of Looking at a Blackbird" by Wallace Stevens
"More Than Enough" by Marge Piercy

Cities, States and Countries
"Chicago" by Carl Sandburg
"A Supermarket in California" by Allen Ginsberg
"Crossing Brooklyn Ferry" by Walt Whitman
"Harlem" by Langston Hughes
"Urban Renewal" by Yusef Komunyakaa

Passing of Time
Book 1, Ode 11 (Carpe Diem) by Horace
"To His Coy Mistress" by Andrew Marvell
"Arise, Go Down" by Li-Young Lee
"Be Drunk" by Charles Baudelaire
"Spring and Fall: To A Young Child" by Gerard Manley Hopkins
"1994" by Lucille Clifton

Chapter 3:
Seeming Free but Fettered Fast

Andrea del Sarto
Robert Browning

The last monk leaves the garden; days decrease,
And autumn grows, autumn in everything.
Eh? the whole seems to fall into a shape
As if I saw alike my work and self
And all that I was born to be and do,
A twilight-piece. Love, we are in God's hand.
How strange now, looks the life he makes us lead;
So free we seem, so fettered fast we are!

(lines 44-51)

The Nature of Poetic Forms

As is painting, so is poetry.
—Horace, *Ars Poetica*

I am not a painter, I am a poet.
Why? I think I would rather be
a painter, but I am not.
—From "Why I Am
Not A Painter," by
Frank O'Hara,
Collected Poems

Like paintings, poems can and do follow specific rules. As in painting, in the last hundred years or so the rules of poetry have really opened up a lot. There was a time when people thought the best imitation of life yielded the best painting, until the Cubists and Abstract Expressionists made space for painting that wasn't even trying to be imitation, it was just its own thing.

When poets sit down to write, they have the option of following a form. A **form** is a pattern for making the poem.

Some forms come with rules about the number of lines, line length, rhyme scheme, meter, refrain.

Some forms, such as the ode and the elegy, can only be written about specific themes.

Other forms, like spoken word, have a distinctive approach to both theme and delivery.

One form, free verse, is really a non-form, and might be the most popular type of poetry written today.

In the twentieth century, the use of strict form fell out of favor as poets felt liberated to write without rules. There is plenty of contemporary poetry that defies classification, or that subverts or reinterprets form. However, today many poets still turn to forms, some quite ancient, when writing.

Why?

Using a specific form connects a poem to the history of that form, and to the wider history of poetry. Plus the challenge of making ideas fit into a rigorous pattern, forces a poet to control language, to be delicate, studied, and precise.

Although all over the world, there are probably hundreds of poetic forms, we are going to look at thirteen of the most important forms in English literature.

Although there are many genres and sub-genres of poetry, let's look the three types of poetry introduced by Aristotle: Dramatic, Epic and Lyric. We've seen Artistotle's definitions; today these categories are a little broader.

Dramatic poetry, or dramatic verse, mainly refers to plays written in poetic form. Ancient Greek plays were all written as, and considered to be, types of poetry, as were Sanskrit drama and Japanese Noh theater. The plays of Shakespeare, with their strict meter and occasional rhyme, are also considered dramatic poetry, but in the nineteenth century, playwrights adopted a more natural style of dialogue, and the use of dramatic verse fell out of favor.

Epic, or **narrative** poetry tells a story, but unlike dramatic poetry it isn't intended to be performed onstage.

Lyric poetry is usually written in the first person and focuses on emotions or ideas. It often has a strict meter and/or rhyme scheme, although some contemporary free-verse poetry might be considered lyric.

Another way to categorize a poetic form is through its history. Let's look at some of the oldest forms of poetry first.

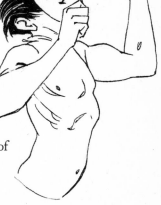

Ancient Forms: Epics, Odes and Elegies

Epics

The epic is a very long narrative poem focusing on heroic deeds, long journeys, mythology and important events. The earliest recorded poems were epics, that passed from an oral tradition organically into the written word. Ancient epics focused on a cultural hero, like Odysseus in the *Odyssey*, or explored the mythological and religious universe of a culture, like the *Mahābhārata*. They often contain lineages, histories, and interactions between humans and deities, and the poet usually identifies himself as only the recorder of events, outside the true action.

Since the advent of writing, epic poems have copied the ancient styles, such as Virgil's *Aeneid*, *Metamorphoses* by Ovid, Dante's *Divine Comedy* and *Paradise Lost* by John Milton. Later epics such as *The Prelude* by William Wordsworth and *Cantos* by Ezra Pound play with the aspects of the epic, inserting the poet into the center of the action, and describing more ordinary events. Because of their length and the amount of time required to write them (it took Wordsworth forty-five years to complete his, and Pound over sixty) epics are not a common form of poetry today.

Odes

Odes are lyric poems of contemplation and praise. The ode praises its subject, contemplates its uses and nature. The word "ode" comes from the ancient Greek word for song; ancient versions of odes followed complex rhythmic patterns and were often meant to be sung, accompanied by music and dancers. Ancient Romans borrowed the form from the Greeks, and got rid of the instruments and the dancing girls.

Among the most famous ancient ode writers was Horace, poet and soldier in the first century BCE. Horace wrote odes to friendship, drinking, and beauty, and famously to living in the present.

Odes, Book 1, Number 11

Ask not ('tis forbidden knowledge), what our destined term of years,
Mine and yours; nor scan the tables of your Babylonish seers.
Better far to bear the future, my Leuconoe, like the past,
Whether Jove has many winters yet to give, or this our last;
THIS, that makes the Tyrrhene billows spend their strength against
    the shore.
Strain your wine and prove your wisdom; life is short; should hope
    be more?
In the moment of our talking, envious time has ebb'd away.
Seize the present; trust to-morrow e'en as little as you may.

trans. John Conington

Odes may be written about object, ideas, emotions, places, weather and people. Contemporary odes don't have a set rhyme or rhythmic pattern. The Chilean poet Pablo Neruda wrote a number of odes to common things, including tuna fish, cats, salt and artichokes. In his poem, "Ode to My Socks," he writes that a gift of handmade socks shocks him with its loveliness and kindness:

The moral
of my ode is this:
beauty is twice
beauty
and what is good is doubly
good
when it is a matter of two socks
made of wool
in winter.

(lines 47-52)

trans. Robert Bly

Elegies

A lyric poem of mourning, most often written to mourn the loss of a loved one, or a leader or hero, an elegy may also be written for a thing, or a time or expressing sorrow in general.

Thomas Gray's "Elegy Written in a Country Churchyard" was written to all the dead buried there, none famous or rich, and is a meditation on inequality in life and equality in death. In lines 13-20, he describes the cemetery and the people he imagines buried there:

Beneath those rugged elms, that yew-tree's shade,
  Where heaves the turf in many a mould'ring heap,
Each in his narrow cell for ever laid,
  The rude forefathers of the hamlet sleep.

The breezy call of incense-breathing Morn,
  The swallow twitt'ring from the straw-built shed,
The cock's shrill clarion, or the echoing horn,
  No more shall rouse them from their lowly bed.

(lines 13-20)

In the last few centuries, more and more poets write elegies not to people, but to mourn the passing of ideas, or the fate of man, national tragedies or any numerous causes of sadness. However, an elegy is still a powerful way to reflect upon a single life, to memorialize and to try to cope with grief, as Theodore Roethke does in his poem "Elegy for Jane (My student, thrown by a horse)," in which he wishes he could bring her back to life.

> If only I could nudge you from this sleep,
> My maimed darling, my skittery pigeon.

(lines 18-19)

Song Forms:
Ballads, Sonnets, Sestinas, Villanelles and Limericks

Ballads

The ballad evolved from northern European story-telling song forms. Ballads are often broken up into stanzas of equal length, and many ballads use repetition, rhythm and rhyme in order to give the poem a more song-like sound.

"The Walrus and the Carpenter" by Lewis Carroll is a ballad from his book, *Through the Looking-Glass* (1871). Carroll rhymes the second, fourth, and sixth line in each six line stanza, giving the poem a song-like quality — and in some adaptations of this book the poem is set to music and sung.

> The sun was shining on the sea,
> Shining with all his might:
> He did his very best to make
> The billows smooth and bright—
> And this was odd, because it was
> The middle of the night.
>
> The moon was shining sulkily,
> Because she thought the sun
> Had got no business to be there
> After the day was done—
> "It's very rude of him," she said,
> "To come and spoil the fun!"

(lines 1-12)

Perhaps the most famous American ballad writer was Edgar Allan Poe, who used the song form for the last poem he wrote before he died, "Annabel Lee."

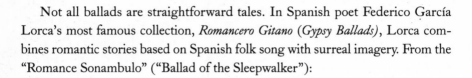

> It was many and many a year ago,
>   In a kingdom by the sea,
> That a maiden lived whom you my know
>   By the name of Annabel Lee;—
> And this maiden she lived with no other thought
>   Than to love and be loved by me.

(lines 1-6)

Not all ballads are straightforward tales. In Spanish poet Federico García Lorca's most famous collection, *Romancero Gitano* (*Gypsy Ballads*), Lorca combines romantic stories based on Spanish folk song with surreal imagery. From the "Romance Sonambulo" ("Ballad of the Sleepwalker"):

> With the shade around her waist
> she dreams on her balcony,
> green flesh, her hair green,
> with eyes of cold silver.

(lines 5-8)

trans. William Logan

Sonnets

The sonnet is one of the most popular forms in English poetry, and, at its most basic, is simply a fourteen line poem. The sonnet, from the word soneto or "little song," was invented in the thirteenth century by the Italian poet Petrarch. In Italy, the poets used the little sonnet mainly to write semi-scandalous love poems. The Italian sonnet has two four-line stanzas, and two three-line stanzas, and includes a change in tone or direction at the ninth line, called a "**volta**."

After the sonnet made its way into English poetry from Italy, it became the most popular form of poetry from the mid 1500s to around 1670. Everyone, including Queen Elizabeth, most of her court, and all of the poets and writers of the time wrote sonnets.

The English, or Shakespearian, sonnet differs a little from the Italian, or Petrarchan, sonnet.

Neither Shakespeare nor Petrarch invented the sonnets that got named after them. But both wrote so many popular and enduring sonnets that they got credit for the forms. If you are a good enough poet, people will probably name stuff after you.

The Shakespearian sonnet is not divided into stanzas and is written in iambic pentameter, or ten syllable lines. It follows a set rhyme scheme of A-B-A-B, C-D-C-D, E-F-E-F, G-G.

Shakespeare's sonnets are known by the numbers they were given when they were first published. Here is one of his most famous, Sonnet 18, which contains one of the biggest acts of bravado in all poetry.

Sonnet 18

Shall I compare thee to a summer's day?
Thou art more lovely and more temperate:
Rough winds do shake the darling buds of May,
And summer's lease hath all too short a date;
Sometime too hot the eye of heaven shines,
And often is his gold complexion dimmed;
And every fair from fair sometime declines,
By chance or nature's changing course untrimmed.
But thy eternal summer shall not fade,
Nor lose possession of that fair thou ow'st;
Nor shall death brag thou wander'st in his shade,
When in eternal lines to time thou grow'st:
   So long as men can breathe or eyes can see,
   So long lives this, and this gives life to thee.

Notice how Shakespeare, after spending eight lines saying that his love's beauty can't be compared changes direction on line nine and says "but."

But what?

But it doesn't matter that he can't find the perfect metaphor in nature for her beauty, because her beauty will last longer than anything in nature.

Why?

Because as long as "men can breathe or eyes can see," people will be reading his poem, this sonnet, and thinking about her incomparable beauty.

As long as men can breathe or eyes can see is a long time to say your poem will be read, although, we're still reading it.

Contemporary writers have experimented with and changed the sonnet form as they see fit. Some sonnets are written without rhyme, or without set meter, with uneven line lengths. They always have fourteen lines.

Poet E. E. Cummings wrote many sonnets, sometimes with rhyme, sometimes without, often playing with spacing, punctuation and stanza breaks, so that the poems barely look like sonnets at all.

my sonnet is A light goes on in

my sonnet is A light goes on in
the toiletwindow,that's straightacross from
my window,night air bothered with a rustling din

sort of sublimated tom-tom
which quite outdoes the mandolin-

man's tiny racket. The horses sleep upstairs.
And you can see their ears. Ears win-

k,funny stable. In the morning they go out in pairs:
amazingly,one pair is white
(but you know that)they look at each other. Nudge.

(if they love each other,who cares?)
They pull the morning out of the night.

I am living with a mouse who shares

my meals with him,which is fair as i judge.

e. e. cummings

By using a well known form and really messing with, and by writing about toilet windows, love between horses and mice in the apartment, Cummings is both connecting his poem to the formality of the sonnet and gently poking fun.

Sestinas

The sestina originated as a hybrid song/poem in thirteenth century France, and meant for show-offs. It requires tricky repetition and careful word choice, and completing one was, and remains to this day, a show of wit and poetic chops.

Each of the final words of the first six lines shows up again as an end word in the lines of the next five stanzas, but the words rotate position so that the last word of the first line of the first stanza becomes the last word of the second line of the second stanza, etc.

Stanza 1: 1 2 3 4 5 6
Stanza 2: 6 1 5 2 4 3
Stanza 3: 3 6 4 1 2 5
Stanza 4: 5 3 2 6 1 4
Stanza 5: 4 5 1 3 6 2
Stanza 6: 2 4 6 5 3 1

The seventh stanza, called the envoi, is only three lines, but it contains all six words.

But it is probably easier to understand this complicated form by looking at an actual sestina. Here are the first two stanza's of "Sestina" by Algernon Charles Swinburne with the six words of the envoi—day, light, night, way, may, delight—in bold.

I saw my soul at rest upon a **day**
As a bird sleeping in the nest of **night**,
Among soft leaves that give the starlight **way**
To touch its wings but not its eyes with **light**;
So that it knew as one in visions **may**,
And knew not as men waking, of **delight**.

This was the measure of my soul's **delight**;
It had no power of joy to fly by **day**,
Nor part in the large lordship of the **light**;
But in a secret moon-beholden **way**
Had all its will of dreams and pleasant **night**,
And all the love and life that sleepers **may**.

(lines 1-12)

The sestina has been embraced by twentieth century writers like Ezra Pound, John Ashbery, and Elizabeth Bishop, among others. The website of the literary magazine *McSweeney's*, mcsweeneys.net, for many years published modern, funny and really skillful sestinas, and still has an archive of their best.

Villanelles

Another tricky form from France, the villanelle is all about repetition and rhyme. Villanelles are made of five three-line stanzas and one four-line stanza. The first line and third line of each stanza rhyme, so do the middle lines of each stanza rhyme, so there are only two rhyme sounds in the poem. The first and last lines of the first stanza become the alternating first and last lines of stanzas two, three and four, and the last two lines of the poems.

Here. See what we mean:

Do Not Go Gentle into That Good Night
Dylan Thomas

Do not go gentle into that good night,
Old age should burn and rave at close of day;
Rage, rage against the dying of the light.

Though wise men at their end know dark is right,
Because their words had forked no lightning they
Do not go gentle into that good night.

Good men, the last wave by, crying how bright
Their frail deeds might have danced in a green bay,
Rage, rage against the dying of the light.

Wild men who caught and sang the sun in flight,
And learned, too late, they grieved it on its way,
Do not go gentle into that good night.

Grave men, near death, who see with blinding sight
Blind eyes could blaze like meteors and be gay,
Rage, rage against the dying of the light.

And you, my father, there on the sad height,
Curse, bless, me now with your fierce tears, I pray.
Do not go gentle into that good night.
Rage, rage against the dying of the light.

Limericks

A limerick is always five lines, with a set AABBA rhyme pattern, with the first, second and fifth line having the same meter and length, and the third and forth lines being slightly shorter.

Although there is a town in Ireland called Limerick, the connection between the poetic form and the place is not clear.

Often humorous, mostly bawdy, the limerick dates back to at least the thirteenth century, and may have originated as a drinking song or party game. Shakespeare include a limerick in *Othello*, which the character Iago claims he learned in a bar in England, (a canakin here is a metal cup):

> And let me the canakin clink, clink;
> And let me the canakin clink
> A soldier's a man;
> A life's but a span;
> Why, then, let a soldier drink.

The limerick was popularized as a poetic form by Edward Lear in the late nineteenth century, when he published a book of over 200 humorous and nonsensical limericks. Many of Lear's limericks used the "There was a [man, old man, lady, etc..] ..." formula for the first line, which is still a popular way to start a limerick. Here is Lear's limerick number 12:

> There was a Young Lady whose chin,
> Resembled the point of a pin:
> So she had it made sharp,
> And purchased a harp,
> And played several tunes with her chin.

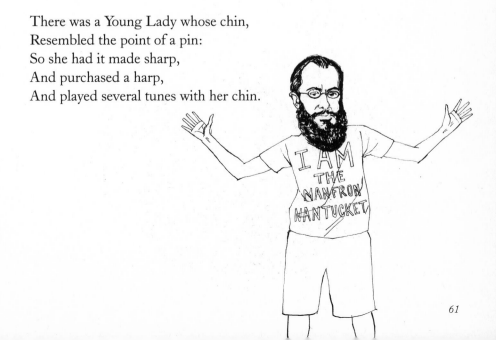

Non-Western Forms: Ghazals, Pantoums and Haiku

Ghazals

The ghazal is a sixth century form of poetry originally found on the Arabian peninsula, which spread with Islam to become one of the most popular forms for poems in the Islamic world. Ghazals are widely written in Arabic, Persian, Turkish and Urdu, and came into English poetry when the Persian poet Hafez was translated into English in the late eighteenth century.

The ghazal has no fixed length, though it is usually between ten and twenty lines. Instead of rhyme, the ghazal relies on repeated words at the end of the line, called the radif. Lines are arranged in couplets — in the first couplet the last words are the same, in the following couplets the last word or words of the first two lines are also the last word or words of the second line of the couplet.

Maybe it is easier to see than to explain.

Here are the first four lines of Agha Shahid Ali's ghazal "Even the rain," where "Even the rain" is the radif.

> What will suffice for a true-love knot? Even the rain?
> But he has bought grief's lottery, bought even the rain.
>
> "our glosses / wanting in this world" "Can you remember?"
> Anyone! "when we thought / the poets taught" even the rain?

(lines 1-4)

Pantoums

A Malaysian poem introduced to the West by Victor Hugo when he included a Malay pantoum, transcribed in French by Ernest Fouinet in the end notes of his 1829 book *Les Orientales*.

It is an incredibly complex poem based on four line stanzas of cyclically repeating lines. The poems consist of a series of quatrains rhyming ABAB in which the second and fourth lines of a quatrain recur as the first and third lines in the succeeding quatrain; each quatrain introduces a new second rhyme as BCBC, CDCD as follows:

> Line 1
> Line 2
> Line 3
> Line 4
>
> Line 5 (repeat of line 2)
> Line 6
> Line 7 (repeat of line 4)
> Line 8
>
> Line 9 (repeat of line 6)
> Line 10
> Line 11 (repeat of line 8)
> Line 12

Harmonie Du Soir (Evening Harmony)
Charles Baudelaire

Voici venir le temps

Now is the hour when, swinging in the breeze,
Each flower, like a censer, sheds its sweet.
The air is full of scents and melodies,
O languorous waltz! O swoon of dancing feet!
Each flower, like a censer, sheds its sweet,

The violins are like sad souls that cry,
O languorous waltz! O swoon of dancing feet!
A shrine of Death and Beauty is the sky.

The violins are like sad souls that cry,
Poor souls that hate the vast black night of Death;
A shrine of Death and Beauty is the sky.
Drowned in red blood, the Sun gives up his breath.
This soul that hates the vast black night of Death
Takes all the luminous past back tenderly. .
Drowned in red blood, the Sun gives up his breath.
Thine image like a monstrance shines in me.

trans. Lord Alfred Bruce Douglas

Haiku

This three line poem came into English poetry in the nineteenth century, around the same time it was given the name haiku in Japan.

Although the form haiku wasn't named until the 19th century, it originates from a medieval Japanese poem called a **renga**. A renga is a collaborative poem, usually written by four or more people, and consists alternating three line and two line stanzas, with 5-7-5 and 7-7 syllable counts. Because Japanese poetry does not have rhyme, is relies heavily on rhythm or meter.

Medieval Japanese renga were often written at parties, with each guest writing a verse in turns, trying to link their verse to the previous one. The poets intended their verse to display their talent and their wit, and like limericks, the subjects were often vulgar and the writing full of puns and double entendres — an excellent renga verse would both display the writer's sense of humor and be a comeback to the verse before.

Over time the renga became more refined, less funny, less dirty. In the seventeenth century, Matsuo Bashō began writing the opening 5-7-5 syllable verse of the renga as a poem on its own. The poems were given the name haiku by Masaoka Shiki, and were popularized in English by Japanese-American writer Yoné Noguchi and poet Ezra Pound.

Japanese Hokkus
Yone Noguchi

1
Suppose the stars
Fall and break?– Do they ever sound
Like my own love song.

Of course, translating haiku from Japanese and keeping the syllable count is nearly impossible. Here is a famous poem by Masaoka Shiki, translated by Harry Behn:

What a wonderful
day! No one in the village
doing anything.

When people write haiku in English, the most popular aspect of the form is the 5-7-5 syllable count; however, the form in Japanese is a little more complex than that. The poem also relies heavily on imagery from nature, seasonal references, and an unexpected twist or new direction in the last line. Which is quite a lot to do in a tiny little three line poem.

Many poets, including Pound and Noguchi, were more interested in the visual aspects of the haiku than the syllable count, and so the form in English is much more relaxed than it is in Japanese. Ezra Pound considered this, one of his most famous poems, a haiku.

In A Station of the Metro

The apparition of these faces in the crowd;
Petals on a wet, black bough.

Even though it does not follow the line or syllable count, it is in the haiku tradition.

Mostly Modern Forms: Concrete Poetry, Prose Poetry, Free Verse and Spoken Word Poetry

Concrete Poetry

Concrete poetry, or visual poetry, is poetry that is literally "like a painting" because it forms an image or an interesting shape on the page. The term was coined in the 1950s, but there were numerous experimentations in shape poetry in the past.

In the 1633, George Herbert published his poem "Easter Wings" where each stanza is in the approximate shape of a bird:

EASTER-WINGS

LORD, who createdst man in wealth and store,
Though foolishly he lost the same,
Decaying more and more,
Till he became
Most poor:
With thee
O let me rise
As larks, harmoniously,
And sing this day thy victories:
Then shall the fall further the flight in me.

(lines 1-10)

Although some concrete poems pre-date the typewriter, this piece of machinery allowed poets to see what their poetry might look like printed on the page. Poets like the French Surrealist Guillaume Apollinaire and the American E. E. Cummings experimented with the shape of the poem on the page, defying the rules of ordinary typing and alignment.

The typewriter also allowed poets to write poetry in the shape of the subject of the poem. One of the most famous examples of this kind of poetry is "Swan and Shadow" by John Hollander, where the poem takes the shape of a swan and the swan's reflection on water.

                    Dusk
                 Above the
            water hang the
                    loud
                    flies
                    Here
                    O so
                    gray
                    then
                 What   A pale signal will appear
                 When   Soon before its shadow fades
                Where   Here in this pool of opened eye
               In us   No Upon us As at the very edges
        of where we take shape in the dark air
            this object bares its image awakening
             ripples of recognition that will
                brush darkness up into light
even after this bird this hour both drift by atop the perfect sad instant now
                already passing out of sight
              toward yet-untroubled reflection
            this image bears its object darkening
          into memorial shades Scattered bits of
            light   No of water Or something across
            water   Breaking up No Being regathered
            soon   Yet by then a swan will have
            gone   Yes out of mind into what
                    vast
                    pale
                    hush
                    of a
                    place
                    past
         sudden dark as
            if a swan
                    sang

Prose Poetry

Prose poetry is poetry which is written in paragraph form. The prose poem gives up one of poetry's most important aspects — the look of the poem — and therefore has to rely more heavily on the sound of the poem, and on figurative language.

The nineteenth century French poet Charles Baudelaire experimented with prose poetry in order to blur the boundaries between prose and poem. In his collection of prose poems called *Paris Spleen* is one of his most quoted poems, "Be Drunk":

Be always drunken. Nothing else matters: that is the only question. If you would not feel the horrible burden of Time weighing on your shoulders and crushing you to the earth, be drunken continually.

Drunken with what? With wine, with poetry, or with virtue, as you will. But be drunken.

trans. Arthur Symons

Allen Ginsberg wrote one of the most famous twentieth century prose poems, "A Supermarket in California," in which he only made line breaks at the end of sentences, the way a prose writer would break at the end of a paragraph. He gives a shout out to Walt Whitman, among others, in the poem:

I saw you, Walt Whitman, childless, lonely old grubber, poking among the meats in the refrigerator and eyeing the grocery boys.

I heard you asking questions of each: Who killed the pork chops? What price bananas? Are you my Angel?

(lines 8-11)

Free Verse

Just as prose poetry gives up line breaks, free verse abandons all the rules of form and lets poets do whatever they want on the page.

Free verse is poetry without a rhyme scheme, or a metrical pattern, or a set number of lines or stanzas, although poets often make up rules for their own poems. Free verse really has no form at all, and it is probably the most popular form of poetry over the last hundred years.

In the nineteenth century, Walt Whitman wrote much of his poetry without conforming to any regular rhyme or meter patterns and is considered the father of free-verse poetry.

When I Heard the Learn'd Astronomer
Walt Whitman

When I heard the learn'd astronomer,
When the proofs, the figures, were ranged in columns before me,
When I was shown the charts and diagrams, to add, divide,
and measure them,
When I sitting heard the astronomer where he lectured with
much applause in the lecture-room,
How soon unaccountable I became tired and sick,
Till rising and gliding out I wander'd off by myself,
In the mystical moist night-air, and from time to time,
Look'd up in perfect silence at the stars.

By the middle of the twentieth century, the vast majority of poets were writing without adhering to a strict form.

Spoken Word Poetry

Like the ancient renga and limerick forms, spoken word poets showcase their wit, skill and verbal dexterity. As a form, spoken word poetry can be pretty much anything; it can employ rhyme or not, it can be narrative or lyric; an ode or an elegy. The most important aspect of the spoken word is that the poet be able to convey meaning to an audience quickly and effectively. Unlike written poetry that a reader can read over and over to get at the meaning, performance poets must make sure they draw an audience in and make an impression within one hearing.

Because performance poetry is meant to be heard, it wouldn't really be fair to include it in this book. However, many websites have recordings of performance poetry, including the website of the Nuyorican Poets Cafe, www.nuyorican.org, and www.e-poets.net, a web archive of spoken word performances.

Chapter 4
Each Age
a Lens

The Poets light
but Lamps—(930)
Emily Dickinson

The Poets light but Lamps—
Themselves—go out—
The Wicks they stimulate
If vital Light

Inhere as do the Suns—
Each Age a Lens
Disseminating their
Circumference—

Poets, history. History, poets.

In some ways, poetry exists outside of history. You can read the Dickinson poem above, and you don't need to know when she lived, or who she read, or what was going on in society around her when she wrote it. You can read the poem, the little message in a bottle, completely outside of time.

On the other hand, poetry and history have a symbiotic relationship. They feed and affect each other.

Poets make and change language by writing poetry. They invent ideas; they change culture. Shakespeare, Dante and Hafez all helped to standardize their individual languages and to bring new words into being.

Poets have used language to speak out against their historical circumstances, and have been censored, like the Russian poet Anna Akhmatova, or even killed, like the Spanish poet Federico García Lorca, for their work.

Poets are also affected by what comes after them. Contemporary ideas about race, class, gender, sexuality and culture make us re-read work of the past. This poem, published in 1772, is by the first known African-American poet, Phillis Wheatley.

On Being Brought from Africa to America

'Twas mercy brought me from my Pagan land,
Taught my benighted soul to understand
That there's a God, that there's a Saviour too:
Once I redemption neither sought nor knew.
Some view our sable race with scornful eye,
"Their colour is a diabolic die."
Remember, Christians, Negroes, black as Cain,
May be refin'd, and join th' angelic train.

It is hard for a contemporary reader to think of being brought on a slave ship as a "mercy." We want this woman, who had to put her owner's name on the title of her book, to be angry or mournful. We need to remember it was a daring and radical thing for an African-American woman to publish a book of poems in 1772.

History can change how we feel about poets and bring new poets and poetry to light. Poets who were incredibly popular during their lifetimes, like Oliver Wendell Holmes, may be overshadowed by a lesser known, like Emily Dickinson, in later centuries. Books like the Mayan Songs of Dzitbalché have only recently been translated and studied, despite being hundreds of years old.

Poets of every age have been influenced by previous poets.

Influence isn't always positive. The nineteenth century English Romantics were reacting against the elevated language of the aristocracy with their back-to-nature poetry. A hundred years later, the Modernists would react against the last vestiges of romanticism when they tried to find a more precise and natural language. The Beats would then react against the moderns, trying once again to find a true language for poetry.

We are going to try to look at a few thousand years of poetry both in historical context and in terms of **movements** or **schools**, meaning groups of poets who had similar ideas about poetry.

A note on movements: most movements in literature were named after the poets who were a part of them were dead, or at least after many of the important poems of a movement were written. It is rare that a poet would set out to write "Metaphysical" or "Romantic" or even "Beat" poetry.

In this history we've tried to include people who changed poetry, or introduced something new. It would be impossible for us to get to everybody. We'd love to. But we won't. We won't get to almost anybody except a very few radical poets and movements. Plenty of poets we've mentioned in this book don't fit into this history, but at the end of this you'll find a timeline of poets mentioned in this book and then some.

So let's begin at the beginning.

Two Greeks, a Roman and a Couple of Epics

Although **Homer** (around 900 BCE) might be the most important poet in Western history, very little is known about the man, and whether or not he even existed. The epic poems attributed to him, The *Iliad* and the *Odyssey*, take place in the aftermath of the Trojan war and have been read, translated and re-translated continuously for the last 2500 years. From Glacus's battlefield speech in the *Iliad*:

Book 6

Generations of men are like the leaves.
In winter, winds blow them down to earth,
But then, when spring season comes again,
the budding wood grows more. And so with men—
one generation grows, another dies away.

(lines 181-185)

trans. Ian Johnston

Reading Homer, one gets the sense that one is reading the beginning of poetry. One gets the sense that whoever wrote the poems had a kind of freedom that poets today can't claim. No one was going to call Homer out for copying someone else's style, or for using clichéd imagery, because he was inventing that stuff.

Although Homer may be the most famous Greek poet, the cultural height of ancient Greece took long after his poems were composed—from the seventh to fourth centuries BCE.

During this time **Sappho** (around 630- 570 BCE), from the Isle of Lesbos, was considered the greatest of all Greek lyric poets. Sadly much of her work has been lost. What remains of Sappho today are poem fragments and the praise heaped upon her by her contemporaries.

Sappho wrote love poetry to both men and women (as did many of her contemporaries and later poets like Matsuo Bashō and Shakespeare). The words "sapphic" and "lesbian" were derived from her name and birth place.

One of her more complete poems, know as "Ode to Anactoria" is here translated as a prose poem:

That man seems to me peer
of gods, how sit in they presence,
and hears close to him thy sweet speech and lovely
laughter; that indeed make my heart flutter in my
bosom. For when I see thee but a little, I have no
utterance left, my tongue is broken down, and
straightway a subtle fire has run under my skin, with
my eyes I have no sight, my ears ring, sweat pours
down, and a trembling seizes all my body; I am paler
than grass, and seem in my madness little better than
one dead. But I must dare all, since one so poor . . . .

trans. Henry Thornton Wharton

Perhaps the national poet of the Roman Empire, **Virgil** (70 BCE-19 BCE) is most famous for composing the *Aeneid*, the national epic of Rome. Virgil composed his poem after a time of great upheaval. Civil war had ended, and the new Empire wanted to be both connected to the height of Greek Culture and to forge a new, uniquely Roman path. Virgil gave the Romans a heroic Trojan ancestor Aeneas, who connected Rome to the Trojan war and Roman poetry to the tradition of Homer. Then Virgil let Aeneas fight his own war and start his own city-state. Here Aeneas rallies his war weary troops:

Book 1

Recall your courage
And put aside your fear and grief. Someday, perhaps,
It will help you to remember these troubles aswell.
Through all sorts of perils, through countless dangers
We are headed for Latium, where the Fates promise is
A peaceful home.

(lines 238-243)

trans. Stanley Lombardo

The Dawn of English Poetry

After the fall of the Roman Empire, England started to establish an identity outside of being under Roman rule. Local language helped strengthen local identity and local literature. And as poets began to write in local languages, they greatly influenced the languages themselves.

Also England got conquered by lots of other people.

Beowulf, composed in England sometime between the sixth and eleventh centuries by an anonymous poet or poets, is regarded as the oldest surviving epic poem in English literature, despite the fact that it actually takes place in Denmark and Sweden. Just as Virgil wanted to connect his hero to the ancient Greeks, the British writer(s) of *Beowulf* wanted a connection to the heroic Viking warriors.

The English of *Beowulf* bares little resemblance to written and spoken English today, and so most of us will still read *Beowulf* in translation. Despite the fact that the land is not England, and the language barely seems like English, it is the earliest and one of the most important works in the English language. The poem tells the story of the Scandinavian hero, Beowulf, as he protects villages and drinking halls from monsters, fights lots of battles and eventually becomes king.

Here, the hero Beowulf sets off to sea with a band of warriors:

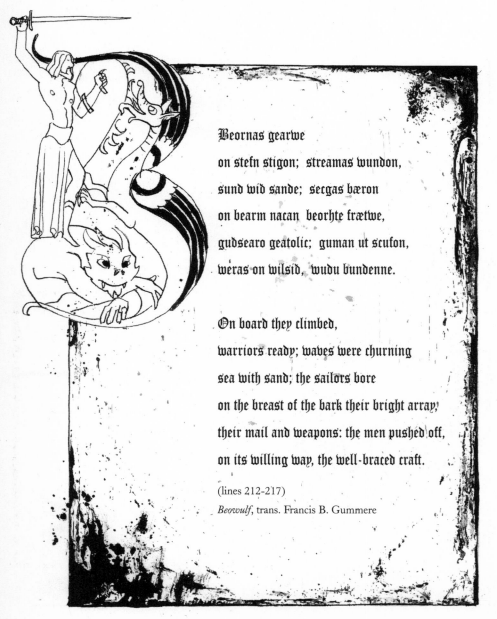

Beornas gearwe

on stefn stigon; streamas wundon,

sund wið sande; secgas bæron

on bearm nacan beorhte frætwe,

gudsearo geatolic; guman ut scufon,

weras on wilsið, wudu bundenne.

On board they climbed,

warriors ready; waves were churning

sea with sand; the sailors bore

on the breast of the bark their bright array,

their mail and weapons: the men pushed off,

on its willing way, the well-braced craft.

(lines 212-217)

Beowulf, trans. Francis B. Gummere

Beowulf, and much of the medieval English poetry that followed it, did not rhyme. Instead, it relied heavily on alliteration and line length to create poetic sounds.

Rhyme did not come into fashion until the fourteenth century and the work of Chaucer.

Geoffrey Chaucer (about 1340-1400) was a well-traveled London poet - who was exposed to the humanistic ideas of the Italian Renaissance and brought them back to England. He was interested in the Italian poets' attempts to reconcile big picture themes like faith and power with the lives of everyday people. He also really liked their forms (like the sonnet), their rhymes and their iambic pentameter.

The Italian Renaissance:

Dante Alighieri (1265-1321) wrote one of the most influential epic poems of all time, *The Divine Comedy*, in which the poet travels through the three realms of Catholic afterlife, as an allegory on Italian politics. Dante called his epic and very serious poems a Comedy because he was writing not in Latin, the language of serious poetry, but in his own language, what would later be known as Italian.

Giovanni Boccaccio (1313-1375) wrote
The Decameron, which is considered both a
poem and one of the first European novels.
The Decameron is a collection of one
hundred stories, ten each told by
ten men and women, who are
hiding from the Black
Plague for ten days.

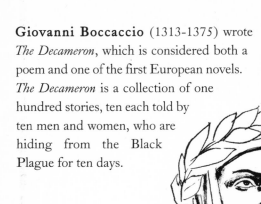

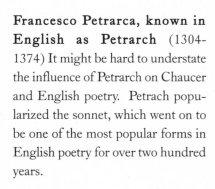

Francesco Petrarca, known in
English as Petrarch (1304-
1374) It might be hard to understate
the influence of Petrarch on Chaucer
and English poetry. Petrach popu-
larized the sonnet, which went on to
be one of the most popular forms in
English poetry for over two hundred
years.

Soleasi Nel Mio Cor
Petrarch

She ruled in beauty o'er this heart of mine,
A noble lady in a humble home,
And now her time for heavenly bliss has come,

'Tis I am mortal proved, and she divine.
The soul that all its blessings must resign,
And love whose light no more on earth finds room,
Might rend the rocks with pity for their doom,
Yet none their sorrows can in words enshrine;
They weep within my heart; and ears are deaf
Save mine alone, and I am crushed with care,
And naught remains to me save mournful breath.
Assuredly but dust and shade we are,
Assuredly desire is blind and brief,
Assuredly its hope but ends in death.

trans. Thomas Wentworth Higginson

Chaucer's most famous work, the **Canterbury Tales**, completed in the late 1300s, seems to be directly inspired by Boccacio's *Decameron*. Chaucer evidently intended to outdo Boccaccio, hoping to write 120 stories, four each told by thirty travelers who meet at the Tabard Inn on their way to Canterbury. Unfortunately, Chaucer died before he was able to finish his work, and only twenty-four tales were completed.

Although he didn't complete the work he set out to, Chaucer changed English poetry by popularizing two poetic techniques – the ten-syllable line and the rhyming couplet.

The Canterbury Tales
General Prologue
Geoffrey Chaucer

Whan that Aprill with his shoures soote
The droghte of March hath perced to the roote,
And bathed every veyne in swych licour
Of which vertu engendred is the flour;
Whan Zephirus eek with his sweete breeth
Inspired hath in every holt and heeth
The tendre croppes, and the yonge sonne
Hath in the Ram his halve cours yronne,
And smale foweles maken melodye,
That slepen al the nyght with open ye
(So priketh hem nature in hir corages);
Thanne longen folk to goon on pilgrimages.

(lines 1-12)

The Politician, the Bard, The Priest and the Puritan

Two hundred years after the Italian Renaissance began and after the poems of Chaucer, the English Renaissance finally came into full bloom under the reign of Queen Elizabeth I, producing influential poet Edmund Spencer, and the king of English Literature, William Shakespeare.

Edmund Spenser (1552-1599) was a politician and poet whose most influential work (aside from promoting the colonization of Ireland) is *The Faerie Queene*, the longest incomplete poem in English. Spenser was a great admirer of Chaucer and tried to imitate Chaucer's style in his work. In his epic, Spenser created a magnificent Queen pursued by the English hero King Arthur to a fantastical fairy kingdom. Queen Elizabeth was pleased.

William "The Bard" Shakespeare (1564-1616) is better known for his plays than his poems, yet his poems elevated and changed the English language. A young man with little formal education, he learned from being an actor, from reading and reciting the works of the greatest writers of his time.

And while to modern ears his language may sound dense, he was writing to be heard, if not read, by regular people, not just the rich and well-connected. Not only did he wish to be known by people of all social ranks, he was also keen to be remembered as a poet. With the kind of swagger and boasting that rap stars wish they could pull off, he promises he will be read forever. And, so far, he is right.

Sonnet 55
William Shakespeare

Not marble nor the gilded monuments
Of princes shall outlive this powerful rhyme,
But you shall shine more bright in these contents
Than unswept stone besmeared with sluttish time.
When wasteful war shall statues overturn,
And broils root out the work of masonry,
Nor Mars his sword nor war's quick fire shall burn
The living record of your memory.
'Gainst death and all-oblivious enmity
Shall you pace forth; your praise shall still find room
Even in the eyes of all posterity
That wear this world out to the ending doom.
    So, till the Judgement that yourself arise,
    You live in this, and dwell in lovers' eyes.

After Shakespeare, English poetry seemed to split into two concurrent ideals. One, the traditionalist trend, looked to the past for inspiration, and the other would begin to stretch and change the boundaries of poetry. This trend continues until this day – poets want to break from the past, they also want to use it.

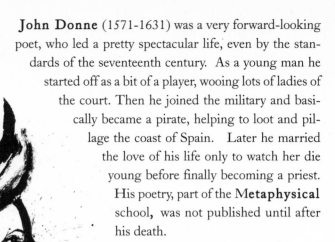

John Donne (1571-1631) was a very forward-looking poet, who led a pretty spectacular life, even by the standards of the seventeenth century. As a young man he started off as a bit of a player, wooing lots of ladies of the court. Then he joined the military and basically became a pirate, helping to loot and pillage the coast of Spain. Later he married the love of his life only to watch her die young before finally becoming a priest. His poetry, part of the **Metaphysical** school, was not published until after his death.

Metaphysical poetry used a range of imagery to express intense emotions, especially love. Unlike Shakespeare's love sonnets, which heap praise on a distant seeming beloved and make pronouncements on the everlasting nature of love, Donne's poems are much more immediate. In "The Good-Morrow" he seems to have just woken up with his wife, looks into her eyes and is filled to the brim with emotion.

The Good-Morrow
John Donne

I wonder by my troth, what thou and I
Did, till we loved? were we not wean'd till then?
But suck'd on country pleasures, childishly?
Or snorted we in the Seven Sleepers' den?
'Twas so; but this, all pleasures fancies be;
If ever any beauty I did see,
Which I desired, and got, 'twas but a dream of thee.

And now good-morrow to our waking souls,
Which watch not one another out of fear;
For love all love of other sights controls,
And makes one little room an everywhere.

Let sea-discoverers to new worlds have gone;
Let maps to other, worlds on worlds have shown;
Let us possess one world; each hath one, and is one.

My face in thine eye, thine in mine appears,
And true plain hearts do in the faces rest;
Where can we find two better hemispheres
Without sharp north, without declining west?
Whatever dies, was not mix'd equally;
If our two loves be one, or thou and I
Love so alike that none can slacken, none can die.

In contrast to John Donne, **John Milton** (1608-1674) was uptight. Perhaps that's because he was a Puritan.

Milton was enraptured by religion, and little else. At the age of 44 he went blind, yet he continued to write, including this sonnet, in which he expresses his desire to serve God despite his blindness, and imagines God needs little from him other than for him to bare his burdens humbly.

On His Blindness
John Milton

When I consider how my light is spent
  E're half my days, in this dark world and wide,
  And that one Talent which is death to hide,
  Lodg'd with me useless, though my Soul more bent
To serve therewith my Maker, and present
  My true account, least he returning chide,
  Doth God exact day-labour, light deny'd,
  I fondly ask; But patience to prevent
That murmur, soon replies, God doth not need
  Either man's work or his own gifts, who best
  Bear his milde yoak, they serve him best, his State
Is Kingly. Thousands at his bidding speed
  And post o're Land and Ocean without rest:
  They also serve who only stand and waite.

Milton's poetic style, like Spencer's, looked to the past for inspiration. During Milton's lifetime, the Bible, the works of Homer and the poetry of the Roman empire became readily available in English for the first time, and Milton himself worked to translate Horace's odes. Much of Milton's poetry is written on specifically religious themes, including his *Paradise Lost*, his epic retelling of the story of Satan's fall from heaven and Adam and Eve's expulsion from paradise. Even though Milton was a most godly man, his Satan is one of the most interesting, and even sympathetic, characters in the poem.

Meanwhile, in Persia, China and Japan

The classical poetry that got rediscovered in sixteenth and seventeenth century England made its way there from the Middle East. As European trade and colonialism grew, translations of Persian, Chinese and Japanese poetry, among others, became available in English for the first time. This cross-cultural exchange changed and expanded European poetry, as poets writing in English found and tried new forms and new ways of thinking about poems.

Li Bai (also known as Li Po, 701-762) along with **Du Fu** (or Tu Fu, 712-770) was one the two most famous Chinese poets during the Tang Dynasty, the height of classical Chinese culture. Li Bai was a Daoist and struggled against the strict rules of behavior that governed Confucian society. He had a reputation as a serious drinker and a rebel—late in life he actually joined in an unsuccessful revolt against the Emperor Xuanzong, was banished and later committed suicide. In the late nineteenth century his work was translated into French and English, which had a huge effect on European and American modernism.

Drinking Alone in the Moonlight
Li Bai

A pot of wine among flowers.
I alone, drinking, without a companion.
I lift the cup and invite the bright moon.
My shadow opposite certainly makes us three.
But the moon cannot drink,
And my shadow follows the motions of my body in vain.
For the briefest time are the moon and my shadow my companions.
Oh, be joyful! One must make the most of Spring.
I sing—the moon walks forward rhythmically;
I dance, and my shadow shatters and becomes confused.
In my waking moments we are happily blended.
When I am drunk, we are divided from one another and scattered.
For a long time I shall be obligated to wander without intention.
But we will keep our appointment by the far-off Cloudy River.

trans. Amy Lowell

Rumi (1207-1273) was a Persian mystical poet, born in what is now Afghanistan, whose works influenced the spiritual practice of Sufism and led to the creation of the sect of mystics known as the Whirling Dervishes. Rumi wrote on the relationship of the body to the spirit and to the natural world, erotic love, the dualism of intellect and pleasure, male friendship and getting drunk, though the constant consumption on alcohol in his poems may be a metaphor for mystical bliss.

Although Rumi is a seminal Persian poet, and his style of writing influenced the development of the Persian language, his poetry was not widely available in English until the twentieth century.

He begins his 50,000 line poem, Masnavi-I Ma'navi or Spiritual Couplets, with the lament, or plaint of a melancholy flute. Rumi writes of the flute's sorrow:

This plaint of the flute is fire, not mere air.
Let him who lacks this fire be accounted dead!
'Tis the fire of love that inspires the flute,
'Tis the ferment of love that possesses the wine.
The flute is the confidant of all unhappy lovers;
Yea, its strains lay bare my inmost secrets.

(lines 17-22)

trans. E. H. Whinfield

Hafez (1315-1390) was the pen name the most famous poet in the Persian language. Hafez was influenced by Rumi, Suifism and Islamic mysticism, and though his work was not well received because of this in his own time, his collected works, or *Diwan*, may be the most popular Persian book of all time. When his work was translated into English in the eighteenth century, he had an effect on the poet/philosophers Ralph Waldo Emerson and Johann Wolfgang von Goethe.

The First Ghazal
Hafez

Fill, fill the sup with sparkling wine,
Deep let me drink the juice divine,
To soothe my tortur'd heart;
For love, who seem'd at first too mild,
So gently look'd, so gaily smil'd
Here deep has plung'd his dart.

When sweeter than the damask rose,
From Leila's locks the Zephyr blows,
How glows my keen desire!
I chide the wanton gale's delay,
I'm jealous of his am'rous play
And all my souls on fire.

(lines 1-12)

trans. by John Richardson

Matsuo Bashō (1644-1694) is known as the master of the haiku, even though the form did exist with that name during his life time. Bashō began writing renga, collaborative Japanese poems, when he was a child and sent to apprentice with an older Samurai. Later in life he began writing hokku, or the three lines stanzas of a renga, on their own. The haiku form and Bashō's poetry were translated into English in the nineteenth century and hugely influenced twentieth century modernist poets.

old pond
a frog jumps
sound of water

Revolutionaries and Romantics

In the late eighteenth century poetry, along with America and France, experienced a revolution.

William Blake (1757-1827) was a poetic revolutionary. He was a self taught poet and illustrator—he made his living as a professional engraver— and was active in radical politics in London. As a young boy he had been beset by visions and into adulthood he claimed he could interact with the spiritual world and receive prophesy. He promoted free love, a personal relationship with the divine, and rebelled against organized religion.

Song
William Blake

How sweet I roam'd from field to field,
And tasted all the summer's pride,
'Till I the prince of love beheld,
Who in the sunny beams did glide!

He shew'd me lilies for my hair,
And blushing roses for my brow;
He led me through his gardens fair,
Where all his golden pleasures grow.

With sweet May dews my wings were wet,
And Phoebus fir'd my vocal rage;
He caught me in his silken net,
And shut me in his golden cage.

He loves to sit and hear me sing,
Then, laughing, sports and plays with me,
Then stretches out my golden wing,
And mocks my loss of liberty.

Blake created illustrations and paintings to accompany his work, and for other seminal works of religious literature include *Paradise Lost*, *The Divine Comedy* and the Book of Revelation in the Bible.

Blake's poems have been compared to folk songs, as they rejected the rigidity of formal poetry of the time. This return to simpler forms, to nature, anticipated the Romantic movement of the nineteenth century.

After Blake, good friends **William Wordsworth** (1770-1850) and **Samuel Taylor Coleridge** (1772-1834) began what is now called the **Romantic movement.** The movement was later joined by buddies **Percy Bysshe Shelley**(1792-1822) and **George Gordon, Lord Byron** (1788-1824) and finally by the outsider **John Keats** (1795-1821).

The **Romantics**, and the movement they created, romanticized nature, mythology, ideas of a simpler past. They felt a kinship to Edmund Spenser's Faeries and to Milton's misunderstood Satan. They favored the outlaw and the outsider, thought common speech was more poetic than elevated diction, and believed that emotions were the truest kind of experience. And most of all, they liked to write lush, lyric poetry.

The World Is Too Much with Us
William Wordsworth

The world is too much with us; late and soon,
Getting and spending, we lay waste our powers:
Little we see in Nature that is ours;
We have given our hearts away, a sordid boon!
The Sea that bares her bosom to the moon;

The winds that will be howling at all hours,
And are up-gathered now like sleeping flowers;
For this, for everything, we are out of tune;
It moves us not.—Great God! I'd rather be
A Pagan suckled in a creed outworn;
So might I, standing on this pleasant lea,
Have glimpses that would make me less forlorn;
Have sight of Proteus rising from the sea;
Or hear old Triton blow his wreathed horn.

On top of their theories of poetry, this group of poets had the reputation of being physically attractive and emotionally sensitive. Their distrust of social mores lead them to sleep with each other's wives, sisters, mistresses etc. and to be bad with money. A number of them died young.

It was the Romantics that give us the stereotype of the poet as a Byronic Hero (once again, be a good enough poet and people will make words out of your name.) That is: an attractive and misunderstood but intelligent and charming man, who is moody and mysterious and has wild tousled hair.

Ironically (or not) the most famous and enduring work to come out of the Romantic movement was not by one of the poet boys but by his wife – Mary Wollstonecraft Shelley's novel *Frankenstein*.

Four Nineteenth Century American Iconoclasts

American poetry had been going strong since Anne Bradstreet's poems were published in 1647, but it wasn't until the nineteenth century that American produced a poet who would become influential throughout the world.

Ralph Waldo Emerson (1803-1882) was a philosopher, essayist and one-time Unitarian minister, as well as a poet and an important figure in the **Transcendentalism movement** in American poetry. Emerson believed it was possible and even necessary to transcend the dualism between the physical and spiritual world, or between spirit and nature – and that that everything in the universe is part of the same whole. Many of Emerson's ideas are also found in Buddhist, Taoist and Hindu philosophy, something Emerson alludes to in his poem, "Brahma," referencing the Hindu god of creation.

Brahma
Ralph Waldo Emerson

If the red slayer think he slays,
Or if the slain think he is slain,
They know not well the subtle ways
I keep, and pass, and turn again.

Far or forgot to me is near;
Shadow and sunlight are the same;
The vanished gods to me appear;
And one to me are shame and fame.

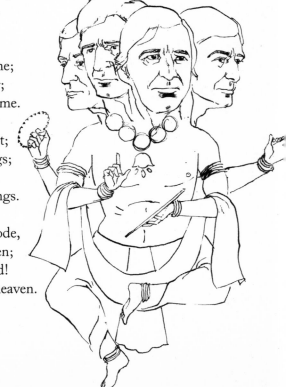

They reckon ill who leave me out;
When me they fly, I am the wings;
I am the doubter and the doubt;
And I the hymn the Brahmin sings.

The strong gods pine for my abode,
And pine in vain the sacred Seven;
But thou, meek lover of the good!
Find me, and turn thy back on heaven.

Emerson also believed that poetic forms and poetic language should arise naturally or organically, and shouldn't rely so much on tradition. Emerson did experiment with form a little, but his ideas paved the way for greater experiments to come.

Edgar Allan Poe (1809-1849) was a poet and writer strongly influence by the British Romantic poets. Poe saw nature as dark and deadly force that might be captured by the musicality of poetry. His poetry takes meter, rhyme and repetition to their extremes, giving them a haunting and song-like quality. Although he was a popular poet in his time, he was never seen as part of the intellectual mainstream of American poetry. French poets, however, loved him.

Poe witnessed his mother die when he was a toddler, his adoptive mother when he was ten, and, when he married, his thirteen-year-old cousin/wife died without ever consummating their marriage. Perhaps this led Poe to write in his essay "The Poetic Principal" that "The death of a beautiful woman is unquestionably the most poetical topic in the world." His poems "Annabel Lee," "The Raven," "Ulalume – a Ballad" and "Lenore" follow his own advice and put a dead, and beautiful woman, in the forefront.

Alone
Edgar Allan Poe

From childhood's hour I have not been
As others were — I have not seen
As others saw — I could not bring
My passions from a common spring —
From the same source I have not taken
My sorrow — I could not awaken
My heart to joy at the same tone —
And all I lov'd — *I* lov'd alone —
Then — in my childhood — in the dawn
Of a most stormy life — was drawn
From ev'ry depth of good and ill
The mystery which binds me still —
From the torrent, or the fountain —
From the red cliff of the mountain —
From the sun that 'round me roll'd
In its autumn tint of gold —
From the lightning in the sky
As it pass'd me flying by —
From the thunder, and the storm —
And the cloud that took the form
(When the rest of Heaven was blue)
Of a demon in my view —

Walt Whitman's (1819-1892) work marked a major change in poetry written in English, and perhaps poetry all over the world. Influence greatly by Emerson's philosophy, Whitman wrote poetry using his own forms, his own language, and very radically using lots of references to things happening in his own time — to his pop culture.

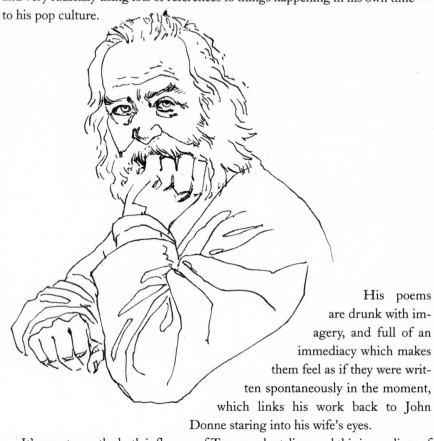

His poems are drunk with imagery, and full of an immediacy which makes them feel as if they were written spontaneously in the moment, which links his work back to John Donne staring into his wife's eyes.

It's easy to see the both influence of Transcendentalism and this immediacy of image in "Song of Myself"

> I celebrate myself, and sing myself,
> And what I assume you shall assume,
> For every atom belonging to me as good belongs to you.
>
> I loafe and invite my soul,
> I lean and loafe at my ease observing a spear of summer grass.

(lines 1-5)

Atoms belong to everyone? Lazily lying down looking at a blade of grass is both a spiritual experience and a poetic one? Whitman's poetry anticipates and paves the way for much poetry of the twentieth century.

Emily Dickinson (1830-1886) wrote over 1700 poems, but published only seven in her lifetime. She spent her entire life in Amherst, Massachusetts, most famously as a near-recluse in her later years. Despite these things, she is one of the most important and influential poets of the nineteenth century.

Dickinson was another huge fan of Emerson's, but, like her contemporary Walt Whitman, she took Emerson's Transcedental ideas and made them her own. Whereas Whitman exploded Emerson's language, Dickinson distilled it. Many of her poems are incredibly short and compact, but her use of simple imagery and language strewn with dashes to tackle really big ideas, gives the poems both breathing room and a weirdness that was probably really refreshing to nineteenth century readers.

I Felt a Funeral, in My Brain (340)
Emily Dickinson

I felt a Funeral, in my Brain,
And Mourners to and fro
Kept treading—treading—till it seemed
That Sense was breaking through—

And when they all were seated,
A Service, like a Drum—
Kept beating—beating—till I thought
My mind was going numb—
And then I heard them lift a Box

And creak across my Soul
With those same Boots of Lead, again,
Then Space—began to toll,

As all the Heavens were a Bell,
And Being, but an Ear,
And I, and Silence, some strange Race
Wrecked, solitary, here—

And then a Plank in Reason, broke,
And I dropped down, and down—
And hit a World, at every plunge,
And Finished knowing—then—

The Twentieth Century and the Rise of the Modernists

The beginning of the **Modernist movement** in poetry coincides nicely with the beginning of the twentieth century, though it was probably at its strongest in the 20s and 30s and lasts, in some forms, to this day. Modernism in poetry was influenced by and grew up alongside modern inventions like automobiles, motion pictures, and typewriters, and modern social sciences like Freudian and Jungian psychology.

There were a number of poets writing into the twentieth century who straddle the divide between Romanticism and Modernism, poets like **Rainer Maria Rilke** (1875-1926), **Edna St. Vincent Millay** (1892-1950), **Robert Frost** (1874-1963), and **Dylan Thomas** (1914-1953). These poets still looked to mythology and the pastoral for their imagery, even as they included American idiom or Irish folklore in their verse.

Ezra Pound (1885 -1972) and **T. S. Eliot** (1888-1965), both American ex-pats who spent most of their lives in Europe, might be considered the forefathers of Modernism in poetry. Both poets were tired of the lyric poetry that was being written all around them — holdovers from the Romantic movement. Both poets were influenced by poetry in translation; Pound by classical Chinese and Japanese poetry, T.S. Eliot by the French Symbolists.

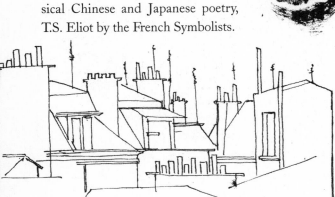

The French Symbolists

The French Symbolists were a group of nineteenth century poets, highly influenced by the Romantics and by the imagery of Edgar Allan Poe in particular. Like the Romantics, they valued intense imagery, mythology and the supernatural; unlike the Romantics their imagery was based on the city— urban decay and decadence are a favorite theme. "Les Fleurs du Mal" ("Flowers of Evil") by **Charles Baudelaire** (1821-1867) is an iconic Symbolist work—it was banned for obscenity.

Eliot, whose "The Waste Land" and "Love Song of J. Alfred Prufrock" are among the best known poems of the twentieth century, maintains some of the lyricism of the Romantic movement, but is profoundly modern in theme and imagery, and uses repetition in a way that unsettles his poems. He wrote about disillusionment with modern life and uncertainty about the future, about fears of inadequacy and ironic detachment from one's surroundings, using contemporary references and urban imagery.

Rhapsody on a Windy Night
T. S Eliot

Half-past one,
The street lamp sputtered,
The street lamp muttered,
The street lamp said, "Regard that woman
Who hesitates towards you in the light of the door
Which opens on her like a grin.
You see the border of her dress
Is torn and stained with sand,
And you see the corner of her eye
Twists like a crooked pin."

(lines 13-22)

Pound was and is a little more controversial than Eliot. He never gained the fame that Eliot had, despite his influence on other poets. Pound is best known, ironically, for his fourteen word poem "In the Station of the Metro," and for his unfinished, 23,000 poem *Cantos*, which he spent forty years composing. During WWII, Pound lived in Italy and sided with the Italian fascists. After the war, he was tried for treason and committed to a mental institution.

Beyond his own poetry, Pound was a major influence on a number of modernists. His friends in included:

William Butler Yeats (1865-1939), poet, playwright and politician, already had a reputation as the major star of Irish poetry when he came under Pound's influence late in life. After making a career in the Romantic-influenced Celtic Revival movement, Yeats embraced modern imagery and language.

Gertrude Stein (1874-1946), who was a little older than many of her male modernist contemporaries, and began writing a little later. She is considered both a novelist and a poet, and much of her work straddles the line between poetry and prose, and between sense and nonsense.

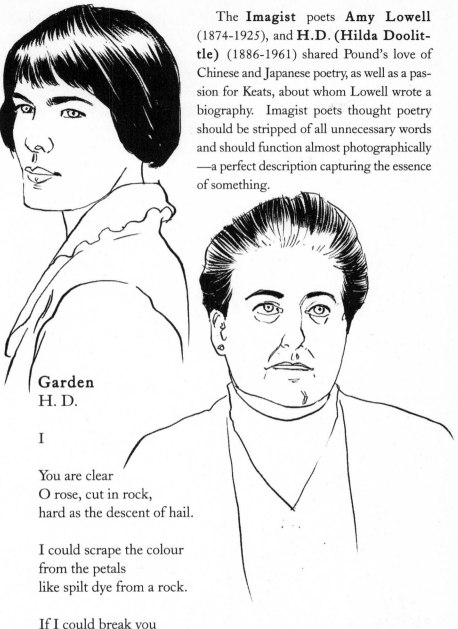

The **Imagist** poets **Amy Lowell** (1874-1925), and **H.D. (Hilda Doolittle)** (1886-1961) shared Pound's love of Chinese and Japanese poetry, as well as a passion for Keats, about whom Lowell wrote a biography. Imagist poets thought poetry should be stripped of all unnecessary words and should function almost photographically —a perfect description capturing the essence of something.

Garden
H. D.

I

You are clear
O rose, cut in rock,
hard as the descent of hail.

I could scrape the colour
from the petals
like spilt dye from a rock.

If I could break you
I could break a tree.

If I could stir
I could break a tree—
I could break you.

(lines 1-11)

Physician and poet, **William Carlos Williams** (1883-1963) didn't go to Europe like Pound and Eliot, though he was both influenced by and influential to them. He lived in New Jersey all his life; his parents were Puerto Rican and Caribbean, and he grew up fluent in Spanish, later mixing Spanish and English in his work. Williams went on to become a major influence on later modernists like Robert Creeley and Frank O'Hara. Williams is probably best known for his enigmatic and often reproduced Imagist poem "The Red Wheelbarrow," and for presenting a more American, suburban modernism, through highly crafted and pared-down verse.

The Young Housewife
William Carlos Williams

At ten a.m. the young housewife
moves about in negligee behind
the wooden walls of her husband's house.
I pass solitary in my car.

Then again she comes to the curb
to call the ice-man, fish-man, and stands
shy, uncorseted, tucking in
stray ends of hair, and I compare her
to a fallen leaf.

The noiseless wheels of my car
rush with a crackling sound over
dried leaves as I bow and pass smiling.

Closely associated with Modernism, **The Harlem Renaissance** was a movement much bigger than a single neighborhood in New York City. Though strongly associated with the African-American economic power of Harlem, the Harlem Renaissance was a widespread explosion of creativity among African-American artists, writers and musicians in the 1920s and 1930s, some of whom also had commercial success in mainstream culture. Probably the best known Harlem poets was **Langston Hughes** (1902-1967), who was influenced by previous black poets like Paul Lawrence Dunbar. Langston Hughes brought modernist ideas of using contemporary imagery and language to his very personal and powerful poetry "I, Too, Sing America" seems to be a direct response to Whitman's "I Hear America Singing."

In Latin America, **Modernismo** led to a new new wave of experimental and Avant-Garde poets, including Chilean poets **Gabriela Mistral** (1889-1957), **Pablo Neruda** (1904-1973) and Mexican poet **Octavio Paz** (1914-1998). These poets experimented with free verse, with conversational language and vulgar imagery. All three were political activists — Mistral and Paz used poetry to explore Latin American identity, with both its European and Native American ancestry, while Neruda became most famous for the original imagery in his odes and love poems. All three won the Nobel Prize for literature.

Movements and Schools Spawned by Modernism

The Black Mountain School, unlike some of the other "schools" of poetry, was an actual School – a college founded in the 1930s in western North Carolina as a Utopian experiment. Writers, artists, choreographers and academics worked and studied in an "open" environment, bouncing ideas off each other and collaborating on projects. The Black Mountain School only lasted thirty years, but employed, taught or influences poets including Charles Olson, Robert Creeley and Denise Levertov, who were influenced greatly by William Carlos Williams's style and the rhythms of his poems.

Similar in style to the Black Mountain School, **The New York School** had no college. Poets like Frank O'Hara and John Ashbery were part of the New York Avant-Garde scene of the early 50s. Their work, like that of the Black Mountain School, plays with rhythm, spontaneity and language based on speech

Having a Coke With You
Frank O'Hara

                                                        I look
at you and I would rather look at you than all the portraits in the world
except possibly for the *Polish Rider* occasionally and anyway it's in the Frick
which thank heavens you haven't gone to yet so we can go together the first time

(lines 13-16)

Also influenced by William Carlos Williams were the **Beats**. In 1956 when Allen Ginsberg got up to read "Howl" at Gallery 6 in San Francisco, the Beat movement official began. It was less of a reading and more of a performance art piece mixed with a manifesto, and it exemplified what the Beats were getting at — liberating poetry from the stuffiness of form; ecstatic language mixed with anarchist politics.

Beat poetry prized free-association, or spontaneous comparisons, to more traditional allusions and symbols.

The Beats took their name from novelist Jack Kerouac, who called his generation "beat" as in tired, worn out. They were influenced by Walt Whitman, William Blake and William Carlos Williams, and, in addition to Ginsberg, included poets Kenneth Rexroth, Gary Snyder and Lawrence Ferlinghetti.

Howl
Allen Ginsberg

I saw the best minds of my generation destroyed by madness, starving
    hysterical naked,
dragging themselves through the negro streets at dawn looking for an
    angry fix,
angelheaded hipsters burning for the ancient heavenly connection to the
    starry dynamo in the machinery of night,

(lines 1-3)

Starting in the 1950s the **Confessional movement** took hold of American poetry and continued to dominate until the 1970s, with a group of poets including poets Sylvia Plath, Robert Lowell, Elizabeth Bishop, John Berryman and Anne Sexton. Although they didn't like the name, it describes their poetry well – they wrote about personal history and self-revelation, issues from their childhoods, relationships and family, often with humor and irony. Confessional poems are highly emotional and personal, often to the point of being uncomfortable. These lines from Sylvia Plath's "Lady Lazarus" were published after she committed suicide in 1963 and in the bleakest of humor, comment on how adept she is at the art of dying:

I do it so it feels like hell.
I do it so it feels real.
I guess you could say I've a call.

(lines 46-48)

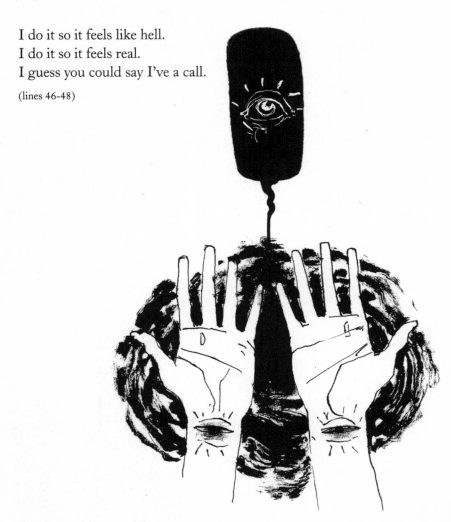

Post-Modern Poets

Black Arts Movement poets of the 1960s and 70s explored identity, and re-imagined a kind of poetry which used African-American language, culture references and symbols. Strongly influenced by the blues and by the Black Power movement of the 60's, as well as Confessional Poetry, Black Art's poets like Amiri Baraka, Audre Lorde, and Gwendolyn Brooks wrote poetry that was both personal and political, and was unflinching in its use of language.

A New Reality Is Better Than a New Movie!
Amiri Baraka

If you don't like it, what you gonna do about it. That was the
question we asked each
   other, &
still right regularly need to ask.

(lines 26-29)

Other Politically/Identity
Based Poetry Movements:
Chicano
Feminist
Native-American
Renaissance
Nuyorican
Post-Colonial

Black Arts had a huge impact on **Spoken word poetry,** as well as rap. Spoken word is poetry which is meant to be read aloud, and is sometimes not written down at all. Oral or spoken poetry is the oldest known form of poetry in the world, but in the 1980s and 1990s performance poetry had a major resurgence in cities like Chicago and New York, as poets began to read or even improvise poetry as part of competitive poetry slams.

Poetry slams, started by Chicagoan Marc Smith, are often open events in which anyone can show up to read or improvise poetry. Winners at slams are decided by audience reaction. Although some slams are invite only, or are national competitions based on winning local slams, the general idea of the slam is that it is open to anyone, regardless of race, gender, class, or education. Because of this, spoken word poetry is often seen as more open to women, gays and lesbians, people of color — people who may feel that established forms of poetry do not represent them or give them voice. Others criticize the competitive nature of slams, likening them to sporting events.

Oulipo or "Ouvroir de littérature potentielle" thought the process of writing poetry was as important as the product. Begun in France (hence the French name) by mathematicians, Oulipo poets wanted to write using new sorts of structures and patterns, called **constraints**. These might be arbitrary rules for writing poems, like not using any words with the letter "e", or replacing every seventh word in a poem. For Oulipians, figuring out the rules and then trying to stick to them means as much as the final product.

BARK!

The **L-A-N-G-U-A-G-E** poets, like Lyn Hejinian and Rae Armantrout, who were strongly influenced by Gertrude Stein, played with sense of words and ideas about the connection between sound and meaning and expectation.

Have you ever suddenly been struck by how odd a word sounded, as if it was divorced from its meaning or repeated a word until it no longer sounded like English? This is the sort of thing, in a more sophisticated way, that L-A-N-G-U-A-G-E poets work on, often using **found text** – text written by someone else – and rearranging it to discover new meanings in the original.

Hip hop and poetry

One of the most important, and maybe controversial things that happened to poetry at the end of the twentieth century was the rise of rap. Although rap is a completely modern form, in some ways, it returns poetry to older traditions oral traditions. Rappers employ all of the techniques that poets do – with an emphasis on rhyme and rhythm, and they are using the techniques the way ancient poets did – to help them (and the audience) remember what they are saying.

What makes rap controversial in the poetry world is whether to call it a poetic form. Rap straddles a line between song and spoken word. It developed alongside, but completely outside, modern trends in poetry. Yet you can read lyrics the same way you read poetry, applying the same critical eye, looking for the same techniques like imagery and allusion. Looking at lyrics, you'd be hard pressed to find someone who could defend the idea that rap isn't poetry. Obviously it is. Some of the most interesting and complex poetry being written today — especially in terms of meter, rhyme, alliteration, allusion and cultural reference — is going on in rap. If you haven't read any rap lyrics recently, here are a few to start with

Blackalicious — "A to G"
Eminem — "Renegade"
Goodie Mob — "Still Standing"
Jay-Z — "30 Something"
Mos Def — "Re: Definition"

It isn't that far a leap from Shakespeare's claim his poetry will keep his lover immortal to Mos Def's in Blackstar's "Re:Definition" that his words will keep him famous, at least for a generation or two.

> Jams I write soon become the ghetto anthem
> Way out like Bruce Wayne's mansion, I move like a phantom
> You'll talk about me to your grandsons

Or compare the use of alliteration and rhythm in Blackalicious's "A-G":

> I be the analog arsonist, aimin at your arteries
> All-seeing abstract, analyze everything

To the modernist Mina Loy's "Moreover, the Moon – – –":

> touching nerve-terminals
> to thermal icicles
>
> Coercive as coma, frail as bloom
> innuendoes of your inverse dawn
> (lines 10-13)

Rappers play with language, the way all good poets do. But rap has a few things most poetry doesn't: backbeats, music, and millions and millions of fans.

What Is Going On with Poetry Right Now?

In recent years, poetry has been heading in many directions at once. Some poets have embraced a new era of formalism, rejecting free-verse and embracing rhyme and rhythm. The poetry slam has reinvented confessional poetry in the vein of the Beats and Hip-Hop. L-A-N-G-U-A-G-E continues to influence poetry in the age of the Internet, where found text is just a point-and-click away, while Concrete poetry is so much easier with a computer.

Pick up a copy of *Poetry* magazine and you'll see that there is no overriding form, or common look or sound to contemporary poetry. Or look at online experimental poetry journals like *Le Petite Zine* and *Diagram* - the poetry may looks like prose, or a list, or smattering of words strewn across the page. Poetry Outloud and Def Poetry Jam concentrate heavily on spoken word, the sound of work, performance and a relationship with an audience.

So where's poetry going next?

Right now, it's hard to tell. In fifty years we will probably be able to look back and say "right around the turn of the twenty-first century, a new movement was born."

That's why in the next chapter we are going to show you how to start writing poetry.

A Note on Translation

While we've focused on reading and writing poetry in English in this book, because we're writing in English, there is a wealth of amazing poetry in all languages. We've included a few and referenced a few, but only in translation. While writing a poem is difficult, translating a poem is an incredibly daunting task. How do you account for rhythm, rhyme, syllable count, alliteration, and word choice when you change poetry into another language?

Some translators work to be as faithful as possible to the original poem; others use the original as a jumping off place and almost write a new poem entirely. Every translation and translator has strengths and weaknesses. We have included some modern classics of poetry in translation for you to start with.

Poetry in Translation

The Complete Poems of Anna Akhmatova, translated by Roberta Reeder, Zephyr Press, Illinois, 2000.

Beowulf, translated by Seamus Heaney, W.W. Norton, New York, 2001.

If Not, Winter: Fragments of Sappho, translated by Anne Carson, Vintage, New York, 2003.

The Essential Neruda, translated by various, City Lights Publishers, California, 2004.

The Collected Poems of Octavio Paz 1957-1987, translated by Elizabeth Bishop, Paul Blackburn, and Lysander Kemp, New Directions, New York, 1991.

One Hundred Poems from the Japanese, by Kenneth Rexroth, New Directions, New York, 1955.

Tales from Ovid, translated by Ted Hughes, Farrar, Straus and Giroux, New York, 1999.

The Selected Poetry of Rainer Maria Rilke, translated by Stephen Mitchell, Vintage, New York, 1989.

Rumi, translated by Coleman Barks, HarperCollins, New York, 2007.

Miracle Fair: Selected Poems of Wislawa Szymborska, translated by Joanna Maria Trzeciak, W. W. Norton, New York, 2002.

Chapter 5: Imaginary Gardens with Real Toads

Poetry
Marianne Moore

One must make a distinction
however: when dragged into prominence by half
        poets,
            the result is not poetry,
    nor till the autocrats among us can be
        "literalists of
        the imagination" — above
            insolence and triviality and can present

for inspection, imaginary gardens with real toads
        in them, shall we have
    it. In the meantime, if you demand on one hand,
        in defiance of their opinion —
        the raw material of poetry in
    all its rawness, and
        that which is on the other hand,
            genuine, then you are interested in poetry

(lines 28-44)

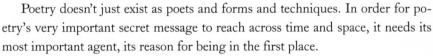

Poetry doesn't just exist as poets and forms and techniques. In order for poetry's very important secret message to reach across time and space, it needs its most important agent, its reason for being in the first place.

It needs you.

It needs you to start reading poetry, lots and lots of poetry, to find out what poetry you like, what poetry you don't like, what poetry moves you, what poetry opens the top of your head, which poems seem like they might contain real toads.

Poetry also needs you to write your own poetry too, because one of the best ways to start getting at the meaning of poems is to start making poems.

We've stressed throughout this book that there is no right or wrong way to read a poem.

Similarly, it's hard to say what is a good poem or a bad poem. Some people love

Poe, other's hate him. You maybe totally excited about the French Symbolists, or repulsed by them. In "Poetry" the modernist Marianne Moore tells the reader that as long as the raw materials, the genuineness of a poem matter to you it doesn't matter what the critics think.

Some Questions To Ask A Poem When You Read It

Whose are you?

Can you tell if there is a narrator or speaker in the poem? And do you think it is the same as the poet, or is it someone else?

Who are you talking to?

Is the poem addressing anyone in particular? Maybe a friend, or a loved one? An enemy? An unknown reader? Sometimes it is pretty obvious who the poem is addressing, other times it is not, but always the poem is also addressing the reader—you.

What are you doing?

Are there actions in the poem? Sometimes a title can help you figure out what is happening in a poem.

What do you look like?

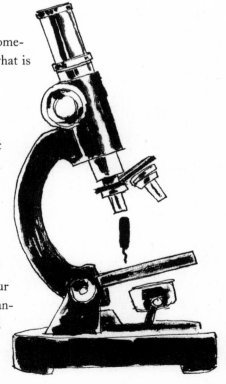

Does the poem follow any of specific form? Can you tell if the form of the poem has anything to do with what is happening in the poem?

How do you feel?

Do you get a feeling from the poem? Can you figure out exactly what your emotional response is? What kinds of language in the poem are making you feel this way?

How do you see things?

Does the poem use metaphor? What kinds of comparisons does it make? Are the comparisons consistent, using one over-riding comparison, or does the poem make lots of different comparisons? Does the poem make allusions? Do you know what the poem is alluding to? Sometimes the internet is really helpful for reading a poem — you can quickly look up allusions you don't understand to see if this adds to the poem's meaning.

What's important to you?

There are many ways a poet can emphasize things in a poem—repetition, sound, rhyme, line breaks. Any time a poet uses a poetic technique, like breaks off a line or repeating a line, or uses rhythm or rhyme, this emphasizes certain words, making them somewhat more important in the poem. Pay careful attention to both the first and last line of a poem, and any time the poet puts one word on a line by itself.

What do you want from me?

Poetry can be about anything. Sometimes poets want to say something about the way they think the world works — to try and give insight, or some sort of new understanding of the world. Other times poets are trying to point out things they don't understand, or hoping that their readers may ask questions about things they may have taken for granted. Does this poem bring up questions? Do you have any answers for it? Does it have any answers for you?

Try to love the questions themselves, *like locked rooms and like books written in a foreign language. Do not look now for the answers. They cannot now be given to you because you could not live them. It is a question of experiencing everything. At present you need to* live *the question. Perhaps you will gradually, without even noticing it, find yourself experiencing the answer, some distant day.*
    —Rainer Maria Rilke, from *Letters to a Young Poet*, trans. Joan M. Burnham

Poems You Should Be Reading Now

Here are twelve books by no-longer living American poets you should read right now (after you finish this book, of course).

Ariel by Sylvia Plath

Throughout her life, Plath used poetry to examine herself in a microscope to examine who she was in relation to others, as a daughter, wife and mother. Published two years after her suicide, *Ariel* is equal parts wit and wound.

Complete Poems: 1904-1962 by E. E. Cummings

Cummings's poems are funny, full of feeling, and with the craziest punctuation known. He was excited about making poems both full of meaning, and difficult, if not impossible, to read out loud.

Harmonium by Wallace Stevens

Wallace Stevens's poetry is the kind of poetry you want to meditate on, to roll his words and images around in your mind to see what you can make of them.

Howl and Other Poems by Allen Ginsberg

The book that started Beat poetry, *Howl* was shocking for its explicit language and got its publisher sued for obscenity. Fifty some years later, it is one of the best known, and best loved, poems of the twentieth century.

Leaves of Grass by Walt Whitman

Whitman practically invented American poetry. The work is bold, brash, and for something 150 years old, totally fresh.

Lunch Poems by Frank O'Hara

O'Hara wrote about love, art, living in New York City, and watching movies. His poetry seems effortless and makes you wish you could have known him.

North of Boston by Robert Frost

If all you know of Frost is "The Road Not Taken" and "Stopping by the Woods on a Snowy Evening," you may be surprised how dark and sorrowful these narrative poems are.

Tender Buttons by Gertrude Stein

Stein's masterwork is both incredibly adept and almost unintelligible, but she makes the case for the beauty and poetry in nonsense.

The Bean Eaters by Gwendolyn Brooks

Published in 1960, in the midst of the civil rights movement, this book looks unflinchingly at poverty, racism and family. Brooks writes using every day language, and her poems are poignant and powerful.

The Collected Poems of Langston Hughes by Langston Hughes

Hughes was not only a major voice in the Harlem Renaissance, but his commitment to the sound of poetry and its performance makes him a godfather to contemporary hip-hop.

The Complete Poems, 1927-1979 by Elizabeth Bishop

Bishop's poems are full of feelings and her "One Art" (with its repeated phase "the art of losing isn't hard to master") wittily explores distance and desolation, separation and sorrow.

The Poems of Emily Dickinson: Reading Edition Edited by R.W. Franklin

The definitive edition of her poems provides 1,789 poems and shows the breadth and depth of her talent and wit.

Making Other People's Poems Your Own

Memorizing poems is a surprisingly rewarding and impressive act. It is also not that hard. Many poetic techniques, especially sound-of-the-poem techniques, come from traditions of oral poetry and from songs, and help make poems easier to remember.

While you can memorize any poem, a poem with a standard meter and rhyme scheme, that isn't too long, is usually a good way to start. Try memorizing a Shakespearean sonnet. It's just fourteen lines, and 140 syllables, or a short poem by Blake.

There are a number of memorization techniques, but start by choosing a poem you like a lot, one that speaks to you. Read it aloud a number of times, until you think you can say the first four lines without looking. Gradually add the rest of the poem. Get someone to follow along with the poem if you can, or just cover the poem with a piece of paper and reveal each line as you go.

Sonnet 29
William Shakespeare

When, in disgrace with fortune and men's eyes,
I all alone beweep my outcast state,
And trouble deaf heaven with my bootless cries,
And look upon myself and curse my fate,
Wishing me like to one more rich in hope,
Featured like him, like him with friends possessed,
Desiring this man's art and that man's scope,
With what I most enjoy contented least;
Yet in these thoughts myself almost despising,
Haply I think on thee, and then my state,
(Like to the lark at break of day arising
From sullen earth) sings hymns at heaven's gate;
>   For thy sweet love remembered such wealth brings
>   That then I scorn to change my state with kings.

You can say the poem out loud, or silently in your head.

Poems with a set rhythm and rhyme, that aren't too long, are going to be easier to memorize, but poems that you really love are going to be the easiest to memorize.

20 poems (and poets) good for memorizing:

"a song in the front yard" by Gwendolyn Brooks

"Alone" by Edgar Allan Poe

"Because I could not stop for Death—" by Emily Dickinson

"Do Not Go Gentle into That Good Night" by Dylan Thomas

"Dream Song 14" by John Berryman

"Dream Variations" by Langston Hughes

Now, How To Start Writing Your Own Poems

The very best way to start writing poems is to start reading poems, as many as you can, as often as you can, and to find the poems you like best, the best kind of poetry for you, and then to just start copying those poets.

Really.

You find out you love haiku and Bashō how would you write a poem about frogs in spring. Do you have something to say about your life, your family, or your neighborhood? Find poems that speak to you and then try to write them about you and your experiences.

Do you love Edgar Allan Poe's creepy, disturbing and out-of-control rhyming poems? See if you can write a ballad with a haunting refrain like "The Raven":

> And the Raven, never flitting, still is sitting, still is sitting
> On the pallid bust of Pallas just above my chamber door;
> And his eyes have all the seeming of a demon's that is dreaming,
> And the lamplight o'er him streaming throws his shadow on the floor;
> And my soul from out that shadow that lies floating on the floor
> Shall be lifted—nevermore!

(lines 37-42)

Try your hand at writing a poem according to one of the forms from the previous chapter. Can you write a Shakespearian sonnet in iambic pentameter, with the turn at the ninth line? What about a pantoum, or a sestina. Perhaps you like poetry that is more free-form, that focuses on language and sound. You could try to right a poem with incredibly compact lines, like Robert Creeley.

Trying to write any of the forms we looked at in the last chapter is a great way to get started with poetry; however, if you are a little intimidated by jumping into a form here are some short poetry writing exercises to help you get started.

The "re-writing the poem" poem

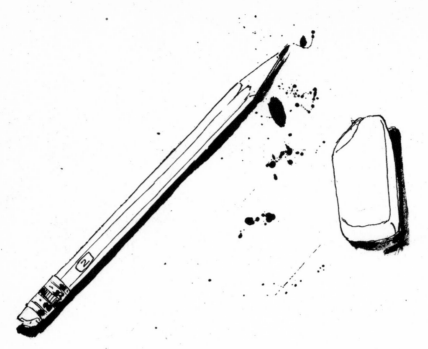

One of the simplest ways to get into writing poetry is just to re-write a poem. You can do this any number of ways — sometimes it is pretty inspiring to just copy a poem, word for word. While that doesn't count as writing a new poem, it can make you think about language in new ways and help you gain confidence to write on your own.

A slightly less copying version of re-writing is to try to write a poem you like in your own words. Choose a poem you like, preferably a short one. It is often best to choose a poem that has lots of good, concrete images, like a William Carlos Williams poem. Now re-write it, line by line in your own words, using images from your own life.

The Anaphora poem

This poetry writing technique is related to the previous one. "Anaphora" comes from the Greek "to carry back" and in modern Greek means repetition. In poetry, anaphora means a repetition at the beginning of the line.

Try writing three different ten line poems using one of the following phrases for each poem. Try using imagery, metaphor. You can make the lines straight-forward, (Like "I am a person") or more abstract "He is the pit of the peach, the last piece of onion skin"

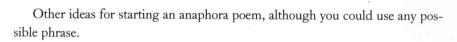

I am …
We are…
He (or she) is…

Each of these poems will make you ask a lot of questions when you write. Who am I? If I use the word "we" in a poem, who am I talking about? If I write about someone else, who would I want to write about?

Other ideas for starting an anaphora poem, although you could use any possible phrase.

Each day…
Every time …
I wish …
I love…
I hate…
Who…
Who knows …

The found poem

The found poem is simple and it can yield some surprise, beautiful, and profound poetry. There are many ways to make a found poem. The idea of the found poem is that instead of starting with a blank page, you instead start with a set of words or a given text and you find a poem in it. Putting limits on the words you can use while writing is called a constraint.

To make a found poem, you just have to choose a starting text. A newspaper article is a good text to use — choose something on paper that you can write on, so not a precious book. If you have a computer, you can also copy a text from an online source.

If you can, make some copies of a text so you can try this a few times.
There are a few ways you can use this text

A cut up poem

Maybe you have seen magnetic words on someone's fridge — this product comes from a pretty long tradition of found poetry. Cut words or phrases out of the newspaper and rearrange them until you have found your poem.

An erasure

Using your text start crossing out words. The more words you cross out, the more focused you poem becomes. In the end, the found poem is the uncrossed out text in the order it was in the original work. You can copy this poem to a new sheet of paper, and decide where you want the line breaks to go.

Try crossing out as many words as you can, but try to keep close to the same meaning as the original text. Try crossing out enough words that you end up with a thirty word poem. Or a sixteen word poem. Find a love poem in the text you have.

Find a poem that means something almost the opposite of what the original piece meant.

Collaborative Avant-Garde/Dadaist Poem

The classic Dadaist poem started out as something like a party game, but you could also do this on your own.

The Dadaists, along with Fluxus and Oulipo and a number of avant-garde groups. were very interested in something they called "chance operations." You might think of it "luck" or just plain randomness. They thought that the conscious mind sometimes made poetry too linear, to predictable, so they like to invent ways to add a certain amount of randomness, or chance, to their writing.

Here's how to writing a poem using one kind of surrealist chance operation:

1. Make a bunch of strips of paper, at least two for everyone who is collaborating — you probably want at least eight total to make it more interesting.

2. Write a number of dependent clauses that start with the word "when" like

    When pigs fly

    When you see a girl walking down the street

    When angels come to fear themselves

    Etc.

3. Write down a number of dependent clauses that start with the word then, like

    Then I will find my socks

    Then bears will wake up for springtime

    Then we will know the future

    Etc.

4. Put the "When" clauses in a bag or a bowl, then put the "Then" clauses in another. Pull a "When" clause, then a "Then" clause. Write them down in the order you pulled them.

5. That's your poem.

Other chance operations for writing poetry:

• Write a bunch of "What is …" questions, like "What is love?" or "What is a duck?" Then write a bunch of answers starting with "It is…" The answers don't have to match the questions. Do the same hat trick, so you get a random answer for each question.

• Try cutting up a poem you have written, so that each line is on its own strip of paper. Put those in a hat and re-write the poem with the line in the order you drew them.

Free-write poem of dreams

Sometimes it is hard to just start writing. We get stuck thinking about what we are supposed to write, instead of actually writing something. This is a good exercise for breaking out of that kind of rut.

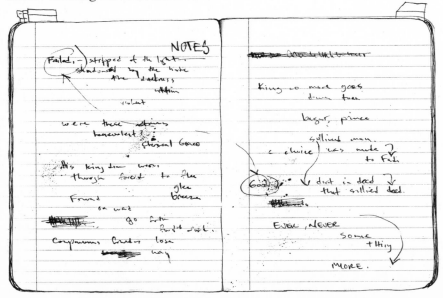

A free write is a kind of writing where you just write whatever comes into your mind. It doesn't matter if you go off on tangents, or even if you end up writing about how hard it is to write. The idea is to write as much as you can, as fast as you can, for a certain amount of time.

A great topic for free-writing is dreams, because they are strange and wonderful and scary. In our dreams we make connections to things we probably wouldn't connect in real life. If you are one of many people who don't remember their dreams, you could try this exercise with your earliest childhood memory, or memories.

You'll need some paper and a pen, and a timer, or clock, or cell phone with a stop watch function. Set your timer for ten minutes. Think about your most recent dream, or one which sticks in your mind. Pick up your pen. Here's the most important rule. Once you start writing, you cannot pause for more than one second. In fact, your pen should never come up form the paper. If you get stuck write about how hard it is to write. If you run out of things to say about your dream, make it up, or just write about whatever comes into your head. Don't stop writing until ten minutes is over. You should easily be able to full up a page.

What you have made isn't really a poem, though. It will probably be filled with good images, with insights and connections. The next step is to turn it into a poem. Choose one of the forms from the previous chapter — say a sonnet, or a sestina, or a pantoum, then use the language you wrote to create the new poem.

The barbaric YAWP poem

Many people start writing poetry as a release, because they are having intense emotions like love or sadness, or because they are filled to the brim with ideas and thoughts and feelings about the world and they want to get them out, to share them or just to record their mind a little and they find poetry is the best way to do this. Sometimes we want to write from a place that is more of a shout than a whisper. Sometimes we want to write from a place that is personal and that comes from our completely subjective and idiosyncratic understanding of the world. This seems to be what Walt Whitman was talking about in these times from "Song of Myself":

> I too am not a bit tamed, I too am untranslatable,
> I sound my barbaric YAWP over the roofs of the world.

This is probably the same place the Allen Ginsberg was writing from when he penned *Howl*. It is the kind of poem you might write when you have had too much coffee and you are staying up late and you think "you know what, I have got a lot to say." It is a poem that can only come from personal experience, and will be filled with images and people and places from your life.

Why not go ahead start with Ginsberg's first two words.

I saw ...

And then think, what have you seen?

What world events have you seen, what personal events have shaped your life? And more importantly, how do you feel about those things? And can you figure out how to use all of the elements of poetry we have discussed to make how you feel about things clear in the way you describe them, the imagery you use.

Revision Time

Revising poems is one of the most important, and difficult aspects of writing poetry. Although poems often seem as if they worn born, effortlessly, from the genius brains of poets as Athena was born from the head of Zeus (Allusion!), most poems are labored over, and go through many drafts before they find their final form.

It is important when beginning to write poems that you write with out to much self criticism — if you continue to write poetry, and go on to share it, or try to publish it, plenty of criticism will come.

But for a first draft, just write. Don't worry too much about getting it right. Try to get down what you want, what you are observing or thinking or feeling, the ideas you want to share.

After you have written the poem, wait a few days. Then go back and revise.

The best way to revise your poem is to read your poem with the same critical tools you have developed to read other people's poetry. These fall into three groups we looked at before.

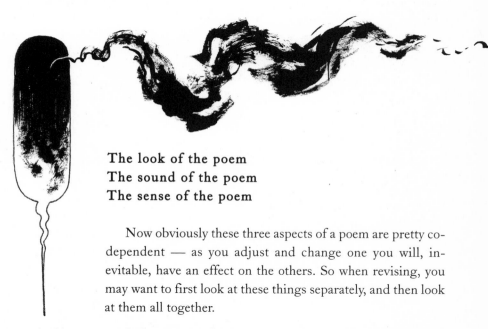

The look of the poem
The sound of the poem
The sense of the poem

Now obviously these three aspects of a poem are pretty co-dependent — as you adjust and change one you will, in-evitable, have an effect on the others. So when revising, you may want to first look at these things separately, and then look at them all together.

And just as we asked questions of poems that other poets wrote, you will want to ask questions about the poems you have written.

When you go back for a revision, the first and easy thing to do is to look at the poem before you even read it again. Think about the following questions:

- Do you like the look of the poem on the page?

- Are you trying to follow a certain form? Did you pull it off?

- Are your line lengths regular? Are some lines shorter or longer?

- How many stanzas? Is there a pattern of stanzas, or are the various lengths?

- Do the stanzas have a function? Does a stanza break come at a moment of change in the poem?

As you answer these questions you may find things you want to change. If you find you don't really like the look of the poem, try changing things — break the lines in different places, change how lines are grouped into stanzas.

As we have said before, choosing where to break the line is a difficult decision, but it is one of the most important things to think about when revising a poem. Some suggestions (but not rules, as you will find many wonderful poems that do not follow these)

- Remember that the first and the last words on a line are the most important. Try not to have weak words, like "and," "of," "the," or "a" at the end of a line.

- Read each line as if it is its own complete thought. How does each line work on its own?

- What happens to the poem is you try to make all the lines roughly the same length? What if you allow a few lines to be very different length from others?

- What if you break only at punctuation? Or never at punctuation?

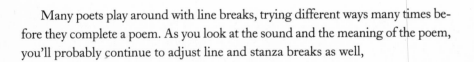

Many poets play around with line breaks, trying different ways many times before they complete a poem. As you look at the sound and the meaning of the poem, you'll probably continue to adjust line and stanza breaks as well,

Read your poem out loud. Read it out loud again. Read it out loud very slowly. Then read it out loud fast. Did you notice there were times that you stumbled over words? Times that you read something that was slightly different than what you had written down? Make note of these things — these are places where you may want to change the poem.

How did the poem sound? Did it have a set rhythm, or a rhyme scheme? What kinds of rhyme are you using, if any? Do the rhymes seem natural, or are they forced?

Do you like the rhythm of the poem? Are there places where you could re-arrange or substitute words in order to have the poem flow better?

What about the sounds of words — have you used alliteration or consonance? Are there ways to use these in your poems? Are there places where you could change the words without changing the meaning?

Do the words you use connote the things you want to, or if you replaced a word would the shades of meaning change and make your poem stronger?

Can you get rid of words that aren't doing much in the poem? Sometimes words we really need in prose bog down a poem. For instance, "My mother and father were married for thirty years and lived in the same house the entire time," might be more poetic as

Mother and father in that house
thirty years they were married.

The revision lets the thirty years apply
to both the length of time in the house and
the time they were married.

What about the images you chose —
are they strong? Do they seem like really in-
teresting images, or are they clichés? When writing a love
poem, roses, hearts etc. are used so often that they aren't interesting to read about any more. But what about monster trucks, or inch worms? As in, "my love for you is like a monster truck, it will roll over everything that gets in our way."

Of course, when revising your poem, you will probably be making changes to the look of the poem, the sound and the meaning at the same time. If may take a few drafts to get it where you want it.

Just keep writing and reading.

Beyond All This Fiddle

The quote at the beginning of this chapter is from Marianne Moore's poem "Poetry." In the first line she famously states "I, too, dislike it." Moore goes on to say that even disliking poetry, she finds in it space for the "genuine" — for truth. Now, Marianne Moore is being a little sarcastic – she was a poet, she probably loved poetry, at least some poetry. You don't have to like all the poetry, or even most of the poetry you read. You'll never know unless you read it.

Keep reading it.

This book has hopefully give you a pretty good introduction to poetry, to what is going on in poems, how to make meaning out of them, what to look for when you are reading. Yet the best way to get to know poetry is to read poems. Read as many poems as you can. We've included a number of poems in this book, from different styles, periods, countries, but not nearly enough. If you want to understand poetry, you'll also want to get a good anthology. We've recommended a number in the appendix, go get one from your local bookstore or library. Keep it in your bag for all the times you have to wait around during the day. Most poems are pretty short. You can probably read a few while you are waiting for the bus or your ride or whatever it is you wait for. Read a poem during commercial breaks. Leave an anthology in the bathroom — but only if you buy your own.

Also — read poetry aloud.

Convince someone who loves you to sit and listen to you. Talk with them about the poems you've read. Read poetry to your children, or your parents, your grandparents or your grandchildren. Read it to your friends. Make sure to read slowly. Let everyone look at the poem when you're done. Impress everyone with your ability to explain the poem, to point out things they might not have noticed.

Memorize a few poems. This will, we guarantee, impress people.

Finally, write your own poetry. You don't have to share it with anyone, but you could. It doesn't have to be great. But it might be.

Go read some poems.

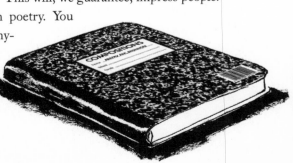

Appendix:

Timeline: 100+ Poets from the Last 3000 Years

BCE

- Homer (around 900): An ancient Greek poet known for his epics the *Iliad* and the *Odyssey,* he may not have been just one person.

- Sappho (610-580): An ancient Greek poet is known as "the poetess" and "a goddess of poetry." Plato called her the tenth muse.

- Confucius (551-479): A Chinese philosopher and creator of the first anthology in Chinese poetry, *Shi Jing.*

- Aristotle (384-322): Ancient Greek philosopher who wrote the first theory of poetry

- Virgil (70-19): Classical Roman poet known for his invented Epic, *The Aeneid.*

- Horace (65-8): Leading Roman lyric poet and Ode writer, he also wrote a theory of poetry *Ars Poetica.*

- Ovid (43-17AD): Roman poet known for the *Metamorphoses.*

- Sulpicia I (around 25-?): The only Roman woman poet from before the year zero whose poetry survives to this day.

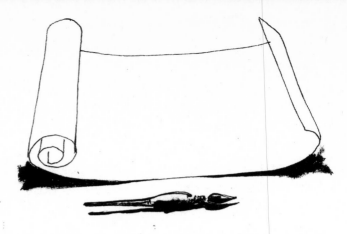

First - Fifteenth Centuries AD

- Li Bai (701- 762): One of the pillars of classical Chinese poetry, popular with the Imagists in the 20th century.

- Du Fu (712-770): Poet and historian of the Tang dynasty, he is considered master of the form Lushi, a highly controlled eight line poem.

- Frau Ava (c. 1060-1127): The first female writer in the German language.

- Rumi (1207-1273): Persian poet and mystic whose work has had a major resurgence in the 20th century.

- Dante Alighieri (1265-1321): Florentine poet whose work, *The Divine Comedy* is one of the greatest in all of Italian (and world) literature.

- Petrarch (1304-1374): Italian poet known for developing the sonnet.

- Giovanni Boccaccio (1313 -1375): Italian poet known for *The Decameron* which is considered both a poem and one of the first European novels.

- Hafez (1315-1390): Persian poet whose Diwan is one of the most influential works in Persian culture.

- Geoffrey Chaucer (1343-1400): English poet and philosopher known for *The Canterbury Tales*.

Sixteenth and Seventeenth Centuries

- Edmund Spenser (1552-1599): English poet known for his epic, *The Fairie Queen*.

- William Shakespeare (1564-1616): English poet and playwright known for his 154 sonnets and 38 plays.

- John Donne (1572-1631): English Metaphysical poet who wrote on religion and love with equal passion.

- Robert Herrick (1591-1674): English poet, Author of "To the Virgins, To Make Much of Time," was hugely influential on the Romantics.

- John Milton (1608-1674): English poet known for one of the greatest epics in the English language, *Paradise Lost*.

- Anne Bradstreet (1612-1672): English-American poet and writer, the first well known American poet.

- Andrew Marvell (1621-1678) Metaphysical poet, his "To His Coy Mistress" is widely referenced by poets today.

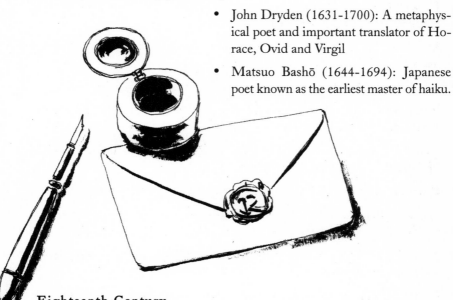

- John Dryden (1631-1700): A metaphysical poet and important translator of Horace, Ovid and Virgil

- Matsuo Bashō (1644-1694): Japanese poet known as the earliest master of haiku.

Eighteenth Century

- Ah Bam (~1700): First known Mayan poet/recorder *Songs of Dzitbalché*, his name means "The Jaguar."

- Thomas Gray (1716-1771): English poet known for his poem, "Elegy Written in a Country Churchyard."

- Johann Wolfgang von Goethe (1749-1832): German poet writer and one of the key inspirational figures in German literature.

- William Blake (1757-1827): English poet, painter, printer and mystic, he anticipated the English Romantic movement.

- Robert Burns (1759-1796): The Scottish "national poet," he wrote in Scots dialect and was an forerunner of the Romantics.

- Kobayashi Issa (1763-1828): Japanese poet of haiku who is also known as "Cup-of-Tea."

- Phillis Wheatley (1753-1784): American poet whose *Poems on Various Subjects* was the first published book by an African-American woman.

- William Wordsworth (1770-1850): English poet considered the leader of the English Romantic movement.

- Samuel Taylor Coleridge (1772-1834): English poet known for his ballads, "Rime of the Ancient Mariner" and "Kubla Khan."

- Lord Byron (1788-1824): English poet who lived a scandalous and short life, though he got his own adjective out of it — Byronic.

- Percy Bysshe Shelley (1792-1822): English romantic poet and husband to Mary Wollstonecraft Shelley (author of *Frankenstein*).

- John Keats (1795-1821): English Romantic poet, famous for his odes, and the concept of Negative Capability.

Nineteenth Century

- Victor Hugo (1802-1885): French poet, playwright, novelist, and part of the Romantic movement in France.

- Ralph Waldo Emerson (1803-1882): American poet, lecturer, and essayist and leader of the Transcendentalist movement.

- Elizabeth Barrett Browning (1806-1861): English poet known for her sonnets. Her husband, Robert Browning, was also a famous poet.

- Henry Wadsworth Longfellow (1807-1882): American "Fireside" poet known for "Paul Revere's Ride."

- Oliver Wendell Holmes Sr. (1809 -1894) Physician and popular "Fireside" poet, friend to Longfellow.

- Edgar Allan Poe (1809-1849): American poet and author of stories and essays known for his book, *The Raven and Other Poems*.

- Alfred Lord Tennyson (1809-1892): English Romantic poet, writer, and playwright who served as Poet Laureate in England.

- Edward Lear (1812-1888): English poet and illustrator known for his limericks, published in *A Book of Nonsense*.

- Alejandrina Benítez de Gautier (1819-1879) She is considered the greatest poet in Puerto Rican history.

- Walt Whitman (1819-1892): American poet and essayist known as the father of free verse and for his *Leaves of Grass*.

- Charles Baudelaire (1821-1867): French Symbolist poet and translator.

- Emily Dickinson (1830-1886): American poet famous for slant rhyme. Her posthumously published work changed poetry.

- Christina Rossetti (1830-1894): English poet known for her book of poems, *Goblin Market, and Other Poems*. Her brother Dante Gabriel Rossetti was also a poet.

- Lewis Carroll (1832-1898): English poet and writer known for his books, *Alice's Adventures in Wonderland* and *Through the Looking-Glass*.

- Gerard Manley Hopkins (1844-1889): English poet and leading Victorian poet.

- Algernon Charles Swinburne (1837-1909). English poet, a late Romantic, he wrote scandalous verse for his day.

- Emma Lazarus (1849-1887): American poet known for her sonnet, "The New Colossus," engraved on the Statue of Liberty.

- Ella Wheeler Wilcox (1850-1919): American author and poet, she penned "Laugh, and the world laughs with you; Weep, and you weep alone."

- Arthur Rimbaud (1854-1891): French symbolist poet, he wrote about the underbelly of Paris as a teen, then stopped writing at 21.

- Rabindranath Tagore (1861-1941): Bengali poet and mystic who won the Nobel Prize for his collection, *Gitanjali*.

- William Butler Yeats (1865-1939): Irish poet, playwright and politician, he started out as a Romantic but became a Modernist.

- Masaoka Shiki (1867-1902) a prolific Japanese poet, he named and revitalized the haiku form.

- Paul Laurence Dunbar (1872-1906) An African-American poet, he was widely published, and influential on the Harlem Renaissance.

- Robert Frost (1874-1963): One of the most popular poets of the twentieth century, he wrote in an American lyric style.

- Amy Lowell (1874-1925): American poet, she was part of the Imagist movement and wrote a biography of Keats.

- Gertrude Stein (1874-1946): Ex-patriot American poet and writer, she was too avant-garde for her time, but influential in the later twentieth century.

- Yone Noguchi (1875-1947): Japanese poet who lived and wrote in America, he helped introduce Japanese poetry to English speakers.

- Rainer Maria Rilke (1875-1926): A German poet, he bridged Romanticism and Modernism; his *Letters to a Young Poet* is a must read.

- Carl Sandburg (1878-1967): An American poet who developed his modernist style from his interest in folklore, and from reading Whitman.

- Wallace Stevens (1879-1955): American poet, attorney, and insurance professional; his poetry won both a Pulitzer Prize and National Book Award.

- Mina Loy (1882-1966) A scandalous American Modernist. Ezra Pound called her the only American poet "who could write."

- Anne Spencer (1882-1975) Harlem Renaissance poet, she was the first African-American to have her verse anthologized in the *Norton Anthology of American Poetry*.

- Khalil Gibran (1883-1931) Lebanese-American poet-philosopher and bestselling author of *The Prophet*.

- William Carlos Williams (1883-1963): American poet and physician associated with both Imagist and Modernist movements.

- Ezra Pound (1885-1972): American poet and major leader of the Modernist movement.

- H.D. (1886-1961): American poet, Hilda Doolittle became known by her initials H.D.; part of the Imagist movement.

- Marianne Moore (1887-1972): American poet and writer and part of the Modernist movement.

- T.S. Eliot (1888-1965): American-English poet and writer who won the Nobel Prize for his accomplishments including "The Waste Land."

- Anna Akhmatova (1889-1966): Russian poet born in the Ukraine, her poetry was both beloved and banned in the Soviet Union.

- Gabriela Mistral (1889-1957): Chilean poet and first Latin American to win the Nobel Prize in Literature.

- Edna St. Vincent Millay (1892-1950): American poet known for her lyrical poems, she was the first woman to win the Pulitzer Prize for Poetry.

- Dorothy Parker (1893-1967): American poet and writer known for her sharp wit and her flamboyant lifestyle.

- E.E. Cummings (1894-1962): American poet and novelist who radically toyed with punctuation, line breaks, and the look of a poem on the page.

- Federico García Lorca (1898-1936): Spanish poet and dramatist, he was assassinated during the Spanish civil war.

- Hart Crane (1899-1993): American poet inspired by T.S. Eliot.

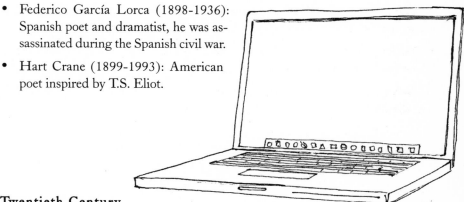

Twentieth Century

- Langston Hughes (1902-1967): African-American poet and one of the most important Harlem Renaissance writers.

- Theodor Seuss Geisel "Dr. Seuss" (1904-1991): Beloved children's book author, he wrote his books in verse.

- Pablo Neruda (1904-1973): Chilean poet and diplomat, most famous for his *Elementary Odes*.

- W.H. Auden (1907-1973): English-American poet considered one of the best of the twentieth century.

- Elizabeth Bishop (1911-1979): American poet and Poet Laureate, known for her wit and intensity, as well as her friendship with poet Robert Lowell.

- Czesław Miłosz (1911-2004): Polish poet and winner of the Nobel Prize for Literature.

- Robert Hayden (1913-1980): African American poet, he was influenced by W.H. Auden, and wrote lyric poems based on his life and on history.

- John Berryman (1914-1972): American confessional poet and teacher, he mixed lyricism with humor and everyday language.

- Octavio Paz (1914-1998): Mexican poet, diplomat and all-around intellectual as well as winner of the Nobel Prize for Literature.

- Dylan Thomas (1914-1953): Welsh poet and writer who became famous for his style of reading in the age of radio.

- Gwendolyn Brooks (1917-2000): The first African-American poet, male or female, to win a Pulitzer Prize. Her best loved poem is "We Real Cool."

- Robert Lowell (1917-1977): American poet and leader of the Confessional movement.

- Charles Bukowski (1920-1994): German-American poet and novelist, his poetry features an alcoholic and depressed outsider, Henry Chinaski, based on himself.

- Denise Levertov (1923-1997): British-born American poet and was associated with the Black Mountain poets.

- Robert Creeley (1926-2005): American poet known for short lines and ordinary language.

- Allen Ginsberg (1926-1997): American Beat poet most famous for "Howl," and for his influence on beat and performance poets.

- Frank O'Hara (1926-1966): American poet and curator as well as a key member of the New York school.

- Anne Sexton (1928-1974): American poet and writer as well as a leading member of the confessional poets.

- Shel Silverstein (1930-1999): American poet, songwriter, cartoonist, and author of children's books.

- Sylvia Plath (1932-1963): American poet and member of the confessional movement. She is known for her book, *The Bell Jar* as well as her poems.

- Richard Brautigan (1935-1984): American poet and novelist, known for his short and irreverent poems, he was influenced by the Beats.

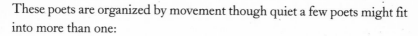

These poets are organized by movement though quiet a few poets might fit into more than one:

Feminist poets
Margaret Atwood
Sharon Olds
Marge Piercy
Adrienne Rich
Diane Wakoski

Irish Poets
Eavan Boland
Seamus Heaney

Slam Poets
Nikki Giovanni
Beau Sia
Marc Smith
Patricia Smith
Robbie Q. Telfer
Saul Williams

Native American Renaissance
Sherman Alexie*
Louise Erdrich
N. Scott Momaday

Chicano/Latino
Sandra Cisneros
Martín Espada
Gary Soto

Post-Colonial
Naomi Shihab Nye
Michael Ondaatje
Louise Simpson

European
Jacques Roubaud
Tomaž Šalamun
Wislawa Szymborska

New York School
John Ashbery

Contemporary Modernists
Billy Collins
Donald Hall
Robert Hass
John Hollander
Ted Kooser
Maxine Kumin
Li-Young Lee
Philip Levine
Mary Oliver
Robert Pinsky
Kay Ryan
Charles Simic
Mark Strand

Black Arts Poets
Amiri Baraka
Lucille Clifton
Rita Dove
Cornelius Eady*
Yusef Konunyaka
Audre Lorde
Sonia Sanchez

Beats
Lawrence Ferlinghetti
Gary Snyder

Language Poets
Rae Armanatrout
Charles Bernstein
Lyn Hejinian

*these poets are a little too young to be part of this movement proper, but they are influenced by it

Resources:

Poetry Anthologies

Miguel Algarin, Bob Holman, and Nicole Blackman, *Aloud: Voices from the Nuyorican Poets Cafe*, Holt, New York, 1994.

Mark Eleveld, Marc Kelly Smith, *The spoken word revolution: slam, hip-hop, & the poetry of a new generation,* Sourcebooks MediaFusion, 2003

Margaret Ferguson, Jon Stallworthy, and Mary Jo Salter, *The Norton Anthology of Poetry*, W.W. Norton, New York, 2005.

Dana Gioia, *100 Great Poets of the English Language*, Pearson Education, New York, 2005.

Robert Haas, John Hollander, Carolyn Kizer, Nathaniel Mackay, and Marjorie Perloff, *American Poetry: The Twentieth Century (Two Volumes)*, Library of America, New York, 2000.

John Hollander, *American Poetry: The Nineteenth Century* (Two Volumes), Library of America, New York, 1993.

John Hollander, ed. *Committed to Memory: 100 Best Poems to Memorize*, Riverhead Trade, New York, 1997

Garrison Keillor, *Good Poems*, Viking Penguin, New York, 2003.

David Lehman and John Brehm, *The Oxford Book of American Poetry*, Oxford University Press, New York, 2006.

McClatchy, J. D., ed. *The Vintage Book of Contemporary World Poetry*, Vintage Books. 1996.

Joseph Parisi, *100 Essential Modern Poems*, Ivan R. Dee, Illinois, 2005.

Joseph Parisi and Kathleen Welton, *100 Essential Modern Poems by Women*, Ivan R. Dee, Illinois, 2008.

Elise Paschen and Rebekah Presson Mosby, *Poetry Speaks Expanded*, Sourcebooks, Illinois, 2007.

Robert Pinsky and Maggie Dietz, *Americans' Favorite Poems*, W.W. Norton, New York, 1999.

Rothenberg, Jerome, and Pierre Joris, eds., *Poems for the Millennium: The University of California Book of Modern and Postmodern Poetry, Volume 1: From Fin-de-Siècle to Negritude (1995) and Volume 2: From Postwar to Millennium (1998).* University of California Press

Donald S. Shields, *American Poetry: The Seventeenth and Eighteenth Centuries*, Library of America, New York, 2007.

Online Resources

Academy of American Poets, www.poets.org

Favorite Poem Project, www.favoritepoem.org

Poetry Center of Chicago, www.poetrycenter.org

Poetry Foundation, www.poetryfoundation.org

Teachers & Writers Collaborative, www.twc.org

Writing Poems

Eavan Boland and Edward Hirsch, *The Making of a Sonnet*, W.W. Norton, New York, 2009.

Emcee Escher with Alex Rappaport, *The Rapper's Handbook: A Guide to Freestyling, Writing Rhymes, and Battling*, Flocabulary Press; New York, 2006.

John Drury, *The Poetry Dictionary, Second Edition*, Writer's Digest Books, Ohio, 2006.

Kenneth Koch, *The Art of Poetry*, University of Michigan Press, Michigan, 1997.

Ted Kooser, *The Poetry Home Repair Manual*, Bison Books, Nebraska, 2007.

Mary Oliver, *A Poetry Handbook*, Harcourt, Florida, 1994.

Mary Oliver, *Rules for the Dance*, Houghton Mifflin, New York, 1998.

Ron Padgett, *The Teachers and Writers Handbook of Poetic Forms*, Teachers & Writers Collaborative, New York, 2007.

Rainer Maria Rilke, *Letters to a Young Poet*, New World Library, California, 2000.

Mark Strand and Eavan Boland, *The Making of a Poem*, W.W. Norton, New York, 2005.

Copyrights and Permissions

Wu-Tang Clan: "Triumph" lines 9-10. From the album *Wu-Tang Forever.* Written by Wu-Tang Clan (J. Hunter, G. Grice, L. Hawkins, R. Diggs, R. Jones, D Hill, C. Smith, D. Coles) and E. Turner. Copyright © 1997 Universal Music MGB Songs, Universal Music-Careers OBO Wu-Tang Publishing, Universal Music-Careers OBO Ramecca Music.

-: Tablet X, Column V of the Epic of Gilgamesh, from *Myths from Mesopotamia: Creation, the Flood, Gilgamesh, and Others*, trans. Stephanie Dalley. Copyright © 1998 Stephanie Dalley.

We used the public domain versions of Marianne Moore's poem "Poetry" from *Others for 1919* published 1921, and the public domain version of Hart Crane's "Forgetfulness" from Hart Crane, *The New Poetry: An Anthology* published 1917.

All poems and translations not listed here are in the public domain.

Acknowledgments

With gratitude and appreciation to the following:

Chip Fleisher, Publisher, Steerforth Press and Merrilee Warholak, Editorial Director, For Beginners for the opportunity to work on this book and be a part of the For Beginners series; The Poetry Center of Chicago, Cassie Sparkman and the students of Hands on Stanzas; Diane Middlebrook an English teacher who showed how to transform and transcend destiny; and poets—past, present, and future.

About the Authors and Illustrator:

Margaret Chapman is a poet, fiction writer, and educator. She received her BA in Comparative Religion from Dartmouth College and her MFA in Creative Writing from the School of the Art Institute of Chicago in December of 2006, where she was the recipient of the MFA Graduation Fellowship in Writing. Her fiction and poetry has been featured in Decomp, elimae, the2ndhand and as a Featherproof mini-book.

She worked for four years through the Poetry Center of Chicago as a Poet-in-Residence in the Chicago Public Schools. She held nine year-long residencies in five elementary and high schools. In 2008 she was awarded the Poetry Center of Chicago's Gwendolyn Brooks Award for excellence in teaching.

In addition to being a Poet-in-Residence, she was a teaching artist at Young Chicago Authors and currently teaches in the English department at Indiana University South Bend.

Kathleen Welton serves as the editor of the *Emily Dickinson International Society Bulletin* and is also a member of the Board of EDIS. *100 Essential Modern Poems by Women* (co-edited with Joseph Parisi) was published by Ivan R. Dee (2008), and was selected as a Benjamin Franklin Award Finalist in the category of Poetry.

She is a member of the Academy of American Poets, the Emily Dickinson International Society, IBPA, the Independent Book Publishers Association, the Poetry Center of Chicago, the Poetry Society of America, and the Stanford Alumni Association. She has a BA degree in English and Italian Literature from Stanford University.

Reuben Negrón is an illustrator, author and fine artist whose work has been exhibited and published internationally. His paintings have appeared in the pages of *Communication Arts*, *Spectrum* and *Playboy Magazine*. His illustration credits include *Las Manos Del Pianista*, by Eugenio Fuentes, *Democracy For Beginners*, by Robert Cavalier, and *Everyday People Can Lead Extraordinary Lives*, the story of W.K. Kellogg. His clients include Anthropologie, Disney, Hatch Creative Studio, The Houston Museum of Natural Science, Nexxus Salon Hair Care, Pottery Barn, The W.K. Kellogg Foundation and the U.S. Open. He is also a regular contributor to the independent comic-anthology, *Rabid Rabbit*.

Reuben is represented by Like the Spice Gallery located in Brooklyn, NY. He splits his time between Connecticut and New York, where he lives with his wife Neomi, and daughter Isabel. This is his second book with For Beginners.

THE FOR BEGINNERS® SERIES

AFRICAN HISTORY FOR BEGINNERS:	ISBN 978-1-934389-18-8
ANARCHISM FOR BEGINNERS:	ISBN 978-1-934389-32-4
ARABS & ISRAEL FOR BEGINNERS:	ISBN 978-1-934389-16-4
ANARCHISM FOR BEGINNERS:	ISBN 978-1-934389-32-4
ART THEORY FOR BEGINNERS:	ISBN 978-1-934389-25-6
AYN RAND FOR BEGINNERS:	ISBN 978-1-934389-37-9
BARACK OBAMA FOR BEGINNERS, AN ESSENTIAL GUIDE:	ISBN 978-1-934389-44-7
BLACK HISTORY FOR BEGINNERS:	ISBN 978-1-934389-19-5
THE BLACK HOLOCAUST FOR BEGINNERS:	ISBN 978-1-934389-03-4
BLACK WOMEN FOR BEGINNERS:	ISBN 978-1-934389-20-1
CHOMSKY FOR BEGINNERS:	ISBN 978-1-934389-17-1
DADA & SURREALISM FOR BEGINNERS:	ISBN 978-1-934389-00-3
DECONSTRUCTION FOR BEGINNERS:	ISBN 978-1-934389-26-3
DEMOCRACY FOR BEGINNERS:	ISBN 978-1-934389-36-2
DERRIDA FOR BEGINNERS:	ISBN 978-1-934389-11-9
EASTERN PHILOSOPHY FOR BEGINNERS:	ISBN 978-1-934389-07-2
EXISTENTIALISM FOR BEGINNERS:	ISBN 978-1-934389-21-8
FOUCAULT FOR BEGINNERS:	ISBN 978-1-934389-12-6
GLOBAL WARMING FOR BEGINNERS:	ISBN 978-1-934389-27-0
HEIDEGGER FOR BEGINNERS:	ISBN 978-1-934389-13-3
ISLAM FOR BEGINNERS:	ISBN 978-1-934389-01-0
KIERKEGAARD FOR BEGINNERS:	ISBN 978-1-934389-14-0
LACAN FOR BEGINNERS:	ISBN 978-1-934389-39-3
LINGUISTICS FOR BEGINNERS:	ISBN 978-1-934389-28-7
MALCOLM X FOR BEGINNERS:	ISBN 978-1-934389-04-1
NIETZSCHE FOR BEGINNERS:	ISBN 978-1-934389-05-8
THE OLYMPICS FOR BEGINNERS:	ISBN 978-1-934389-33-1
PHILOSOPHY FOR BEGINNERS:	ISBN 978-1-934389-02-7
PLATO FOR BEGINNERS:	ISBN 978-1-934389-08-9
POSTMODERNISM FOR BEGINNERS:	ISBN 978-1-934389-09-6
RELATIVITY & QUANTUM PHYSICS FOR BEGINNERS	ISBN 978-1-934389-42-3
SARTRE FOR BEGINNERS:	ISBN 978-1-934389-15-7
SHAKESPEARE FOR BEGINNERS:	ISBN 978-1-934389-29-4
STRUCTURALISM & POSTSTRUCTURALISM FOR BEGINNERS:	ISBN 978-1-934389-10-2
ZEN FOR BEGINNERS:	ISBN 978-1-934389-06-5
ZINN FOR BEGINNERS:	ISBN 978-1-934389-40-9

www.forbeginnersbooks.com